HEARTBREAK SUCKS!

how to get over your breakup in 30 days

Published by The Goat's Nest Publishing

Published 2021, updated 2024

ISBN 978-0-9934876-2-0

All illustrations and words by Jared Woods
JaredWoodsSavedMyLife.com

dedicated to

Chantelle, Lizzie, and Sarah

for without whom, these words would have never been possible.

Would You Be So Kind To Review This Book?

By purchasing this book, you have helped me to write for another day! Thank you! However, if you seek to spread more healing throughout the world, there is a way to assist further, and it won't cost you a penny!

You see, Amazon's algorithm is an extremely intelligent beast that judges authors' products based on many factors. But inarguably, our most significant power comes from **verified reviews**. So when you take a few minutes to tell the world what you thought of this book, the website wakes up and lifts the title to higher eyes, feeding itself in the process. The author has no control over this side of the deal. It entirely relies on you!

Hence, please consider reviewing *Heartbreak Sucks!* You wouldn't believe the difference a single rating makes.

Thank you again so very much!
Lots of love,
Jared Woods

Amazon Link:
https://mybook.to/heartbreaksucks

Chapters

How to Best Use This Book

However you want to.

But here are a few pointers to help you move along all the same:

1. This book was designed to be read in the morning, each day, for 30 days in a row. Do what you can! That's all anyone can ask of you.
2. Once you have read your chapter for that morning, try to spend a few brief moments in your head. Allow your thoughts to swirl this information around. Try come up with a few fun ways in which to integrate the proposed ideas into your day. The recap boxes at the end of each chapter should assist this process.
3. Some days will make complete sense to you.
   The content will leap out and stick into your brain for all eternity.
   Remember those days.
   Conversely, other days won't make much sense at all, or may not even apply to your specific situation whatsoever.
   Do not worry about a thing.
   These instructions were calculated with this in mind.
   Keep reading.

Just Who Do I Think I Am?

Hey, my name is Jared.

But before I sink too deep into formalities, I would like to start by extending my most profound empathy towards you right now. I can only assume that by picking up a book such as this one, you are not having the greatest time of your life. On the contrary. No pain in the world competes with that of the heart's devastation, except for perhaps mourning the death of someone close to you. And even then, these two emotional tortures are quite comparable. In some instances, the death of an ex would be the preferred outcome. It's fine. This is a safe place. You can admit that to me. I don't judge, because I know how it goes.

There's the nausea. There's the difficulty of breathing. There are those empty feelings of inadequacy. There's the question that you will never find love or have sex again. There are the dark fantasies which play out in your head, the ones where your ex is having a wonderful time without you, probably with someone else. And there's the certainty that you are going completely insane, fearful that you may never make it out of this alive. In these moments of bleak despair, do not fear, for these are entirely natural feelings, and you are not the first to experience them. Congratulations, you are human after all.

Now, not to start things off negatively, but I have some additional bad news to add to your life if you can handle it. Unfortunately, there is no quick and easy end-all fix for what you are going through. You will suffer, and you will hurt, and nobody (not even me, your special companion, your best book buddy, here for you through thick and thin) can wave a magic wand and cure you of the distress. I feel like, on some reasonable level, you knew this to be true already.

However, there is some good news too, and that is where this journey begins. It's that I know of specific steps which you can take to slowly untangle the noose around your neck, gradually chipping the stone away from your guts, no longer squeezing them together. Some of these steps are so widely reported that they have lost their meaning, and we need to be reminded of their value. Other steps are so unique to this book that you won't find them anywhere else, and you're welcome for that. But the steps alone are not what's important here. What's important is that you can place these steps in a row to create a staircase. A staircase you can climb to escape out of this claustrophobic cocoon, complete with a set of wings glued to your back. All you need to do is put one foot in front of the other and move forward in the ways suggested. And somewhere along this hike, you will find your portion of peace, guaranteed.

Ok, But Wait, Just Who Do I Think I Am Again?

Sorry, again, my name is Jared, pleased to meet you! Now I know what you're thinking: what makes me the expert on such a commonplace subject? Do I have a PhD in psychology? A masters in social science? Fifteen years of witchdoctor training? A library of books I've written on the topic? No, I have none of those. What I do have, however, is what you have. First-hand experience. If you care, here is my story, in a nutshell (feel free to skip it, I won't be offended):

November 2013 was a special month in my life, as it was when which I had my heart severely shattered. A girl and I went from a three-year relationship where we spent every day and night together, to a breakup where she moved on to the next lover very quickly. He was a "friend" too, which was terrific. Even more terrific, what that this conflict became so intermingled with my social circle that it led to other mutual friends conspiring against me. People picked sides. Withheld information came to light after the relationship, which rendered all of those years as one big fat lie. And what made everything all the worse, was that my ex-girlfriend and I still lived together. Of course, I was too proud and too stubborn to admit to anyone that I was dying inside, and so when my ex asked me if it was ok for her new boyfriend to move in with us, I foolishly said it was just fine.

What followed was a very nasty time indeed, and while I did eventually move out after a few months of hiding my emotional torture, the mental damage was done. I started to get panic attacks up to three times a day, every day, for about a year. I ended up on medication. I cut off a lot of friends because I did not want to be in the presence of anyone who knew her. Confusion and self-doubt overcame me. My mind hardly had a kind word to say to me, reverting to that of a child. And I was sure that I would never be the same again.

That said, one good thing did come out of this. You see, The Great Relationship Collapse of 2013 wasn't my first suicidal roller coaster, as the horrific breakup monster had bitten into me once before. The first time was different, as these things always tend to be different, but the hallmarks of inner-destruction rang loud and clear in both instances. A persistent pre-vomiting sensation? Check. Self-loathing obsessions? Check. Dangerously irrational plans? Check. Intrusive criminal thoughts? Check check check. This first breakup happened around 2003, and that pain lasted roughly six years of my life. Pathetic, right? I know! Which is why, when these familiar stirrings visited me for this second time, I made the conscious decision not to let myself fall into pieces like I did that first round. Not ever again.

And so I lifted my fists, and I fought. I ran straight into the problem with arms flailing, equipped with one strategy and one strategy alone: research everything, try absolutely anything, and take note of which actions brought me some success, as well as those that did not.

As you can imagine, there was a lot of trial and error when it came to this approach, and believe me, I got whipped real bad for the most part. But at the same time, I progressively grew stronger until I learned how to keep my mouth above water and push the distances between the bouts of depression further and further apart. And eventually, when my hazy vision cleared and I managed to step back for a breather, I realised that I had built a decent-sized pile of notes on the topic of heartbreak. Said notes were more extensive and unique than any other I had come across on my quest. And more importantly, they were written amid that special place of pain, leaving a clear paper trail behind themselves, illuminating my exact steps towards relative restoration. It was too good to waste. I had to do something with this.

Do something, I did! I compartmentalised the thoughts and wrote an article on my blog, Juice Nothing, titled *How To Heal Heartbreak In 20 Steps*, published in 2014. The reaction was immediate. It started with some hurt friends emailing me, expressing abundant gratitude that I had helped them to sort their lives out. And then it spread until I began to receive messages from strangers reporting on how my advice had pushed them out of their slump and into a place of recovery. These messages continue sporadically to this day. I was flattered to be a guiding hand in people's experiences because I never had that. What's more, it was cool that my crazy idea had validated its existence, and I mused, *"This would make a good book!"*. Then I went on with my life, opting to leave that whole ugly part of my emotions in the past.

I nearly got away with it too! That was until 2017 when a 10-month relationship of mine ended abruptly *BANG!* Granted, this wasn't the longest nor the deepest love connection I'd ever had torn from my soul, but it still held the painful smelling salts of heartbreak beneath my nose, clearly reminding me about every detail of this hideous thing. And then… that's when it happened. That's when *this* happened. Wait a minute… wait just a minute! Didn't I once claim to be the authority on the subject of heartbreak? Didn't I write a blog article about all of this before? I did! Well then, the time had come for me to put my money where my heart was, and revisit those old words, and perhaps... perhaps now was the perfect opportunity to finally write that book.

And so when the bell rang, I punched first. I pulled heartbreak into the ring with my self-penned manual tucked beneath my armpit, and I weaponised my previous strategies. I researched new books and articles on the matter. I interviewed people who had suffered on this path before. And eventually, I managed to stockpile up so much additional information that my original blog grew a belly and birthed these very pages you hold before you. Yes, I still got battered up more than I'd like to admit, but I landed some solid punches during this matchup, and ultimately, I won by doing exactly what I'm about to teach you.

Which is what I want you to understand above all else. No, I may not be a psychologist or a sociologist or even someone who's particularly sociable. What I am, however, is a person who was right where you are. And from that place, I swallowed all the information available on the topic, tested every suggestion presented, then assembled a tower to get out of the hole, writing the instruction manual as I did so. This very guide you are currently reading contains the exact actions I took. I drafted one chapter a day for 30 days, and I lived by these words, entirely dedicated to the process. Why this is particularly important to note, is because I am not pretending to be some pretentious mentor here. I am the guinea pig of the practice, using my own jagged emotions to sharpen the blade before I handed it to you. And so, as you inch your way along with these words, please keep in mind that I am not merely suggesting you do what I tell you like some textbook. I am telling you exactly what I did.

My main hope for you is that you treat these ideas in the same manner in which I chose to. "What you put in is that you get out" applies to all walks of life, and this book is fiercely included. If you skim this advice and are disappointed when you come out the other side without any patchwork, this isn't the book's fault. However, if you give this manual everything you've got (even if you don't have that much), you will find that I've done my very best to keep each day relatively pain-free and straightforward, and you may be quite surprised with what you are capable. You can win this if you want to. You may even enjoy doing so.

Either which way, I wish the best of luck to you. No matter what your story is, who did what to who, and how much of this pain has been blamed where; *none* of this turmoil is how life is supposed to be lived. Our short time on this planet was never created to be endured as a permanent struggle. And you *are* worthy of moving on.

So come with me. Let's move on.

Your 30 days begin now.

Day 1
Break Down And Be Pathetic

Day 1
Break Down And Be Pathetic

"I needed some space to lay myself out, so that I could decide which pieces I wanted to pick up." — Fennel Hudson, A Writer's Year - Fennel's Journal - No. 3

To prove that we are on the same page, your very first daily task is to do absolutely nothing at all. You see? We're going to get along just fine.

The most important thing for you to understand about this process (and which won't help you whatsoever) is that you are a person with person-insides and person-outsides. It's a cliché to say, but what you are currently going through is very normal, and on a biological level, actually rather boring. Which is why (in an attempt turn your sadness into a brief yawn) I am going to give you a quick science lesson on what is going on here. Pay attention! Don't worry, you'll love it.

"The heart was made to be broken." — Oscar Wilde

First up, we have a cute fleshy lump in our brains called the anterior cingulate cortex, and this little dude is responsible for our sensations of pain. A vital asset! Pain is what stops us from doing stupid stuff! The problem with old anterior cingulate, however, is that he/she is utterly oblivious to whether he/she is feeling physical or emotional pain. This means that a kick in the shin, a knock on the head, or the rejection of a fellow human makes minimal difference. You are going to hurt either way and in much the same fashion.

Next up, meet the prefrontal cortex. This fella has a borderline unhealthy adoration for your happy chemicals (known as dopamine and serotonin) and is notorious for throwing an absolute fit when it doesn't get what it wants. These tantrums are referred to as "cravings" and include the cries for water, junk food, cigarettes, alcohol, cocaine, and, of course, the love of an ex.

As if these players weren't enough already, we also have the amygdala in the middle of everything. Here is a group of small nuclei who wake up during all of this commotion and then quickly press the alarm bells, sending your entire system into panic mode or a blind rage as fast as possible. These little bundles of joy are connected to many magnificent mental health issues, for example, bipolar disorder and post-traumatic stress disorder.

In other words, right now, you are the equivalent of a crazy drug addict who has been beaten up, wanting nothing more than just one more hit of that love you once had, a tiny taste to alleviate this anguish. And that's all.

Which is why… we are going to take things... really... slow…

"Instead of heading for a big mental breakdown, I decided to have a small breakdown every Tuesday evening." — Graham Parke, No Hope for Gomez!

Give yourself this day to wallow in self-pity. If you can avoid the real world, don't get out of bed. Sleep forever. Order a pizza with every topping and cry into the crust until it goes soggy. Think about how badly this hurts right now. Rewatch *The Notebook* or *High Fidelity*. Swear at your ceiling fan until it stops working. Stalk your ex's social media. Stalk your ex-ex's social media. Check when last they were online. Reread their old messages. Scream into your pillow until it screams back. Listen to the saddest songs you can possibly fathom. Shatter into a million tiny shards of yourself as those songs make so much more sense than they ever have before. Hate everyone. Hate yourself. Speak to no one because they're all rubbish. Bury nothing. Make yourself feel sick from the pain. Do not pretend to be ok because you are not ok.

"You cannot protect yourself from sadness without protecting yourself from happiness." — Jonathan Safran Foer

See how far and hard you can force out this sadness. Be as miserable as you possibly can be, and do everything in your power to aggravate this misery. Be the saddest person in the whole world. Look at yourself in the mirror and tell yourself that you are, in fact, the saddest person that has ever walked the planet. Get so ridiculously pathetic that it almost becomes comedic.

"I remember watching the mascara tears flood the ivories and I thought, 'It's OK to be sad'. I've been trained to love my darkness."
— Lady Gaga

Perhaps this is what you've been doing all along. Perhaps this almost feels like a step backward for you. But there are two very important reasons as to why you must commit to this part of our practice.

Reason #1 (and you've heard this too many times before): if you bottle up your feelings, they are going pop open one day, and it will be at the most inopportune time you can fathom. Do not forget that you are mourning a loss like a death, because that is exactly what this is. It's a loss. These feelings are screaming for attention, so give it to them! Admit a degree of powerlessness over your own emotions. Hit rock bottom so hard that your head makes a noise.

You don't need to rely on my word about this either. Multiple studies indicate that our standard procedure of holding onto negative thoughts breed hazardous health implications, such as heart disease and cancer. You don't want any of those, so let's sob them out. Tears themselves are proven to contain actual toxins, meaning that the well-documented cleansing effect of crying is quite literal. You are detoxifying your body just by allowing yourself a bit of a breakdown.

"We need never be ashamed of our tears." — Charles Dickens, Great Expectations

And **Reason #2**: As far as this book goes, this will be your last chance to feel so sorry for yourself. Use the time wisely.

"Crying is all right in its way while it lasts. But you have to stop sooner or later, and then you still have to decide what to do."
— C.S. Lewis, The Silver Chair

And so to recap...

There is nothing to do today except to feel terrible. Your mission is to see just how awfully low you can go. Let it all fall down!

Day 2
This Is A Game

Day 2
This Is A Game

"Life is far too important a thing ever to talk seriously about it." — Oscar Wilde

Hello! And welcome to your very first day of recovery! But before we proceed, I have a very important to question to ask you:

Are you willing to do everything in your power to stop this pain in your heart?

If you've answered no, then I don't know what to tell you, except that I'm sorry. You may have wasted your money on this book. All of the smart advice in the world means nothing if you aren't committed to taking action on your side, and you might as well just keep reading Day 1 over and over until nature completes its course. What a pity that would be. But if so, it's been lovely chatting with you.

"You've done it before and you can do it now. See the positive possibilities. Redirect the substantial energy of your frustration and turn it into positive, effective, unstoppable determination." — Ralph Marston

However, if you answered yes, then you've legitimately taken the most crucial step of the whole book. I am delighted by this, and you won't regret it! Here, hold my hand, and together, let's stand up against this ugly demon living in your chest and beat it down with everything we've got! And this is how we begin:

You need to start looking at this as a game. Is it a fun game? Of course not! It's the worst game ever invented, probably forged from the deepest of coals in Hell by the very hands of Satan himself. But it's a game all the same. And much like every game, there is a degree of perseverance and luck involved. Yet above even this, it is a game of strategy. You have reached a fork in the road of your life, but this is not a dead-end, for you are not dead (even if you may feel like you are). Instead, this is a challenge, or even an opportunity, one which could potentially redefine and fundamentally change you as a human being for the rest of your life. But don't worry about such magical concepts at this point, it's too soon. Instead, let's take a deep breath and start playing.

Your first quest is a simple one. Go and get a paper notebook. Perhaps you have one lying around, or perhaps you need to venture out and purchase one, but however you obtain it, ensure that you select a notebook which looks pleasing in appearance, happy in its presentation. Bright colouring is recommended. A cartoon character covering is encouraged. And while you're at it, why not get one of those funky pens too? You know, the types with the fluffy ends? Those pens are super cool, I used one with a banana ornament attached to it, it was a cute touch.

"Life's a game, all you have to do, is know how to play it."
— Anonymous

Behold: this is your new best friend, your confidant, your personal advisor… it's basically you, in paper and ink form; empty, yet also a blank canvas to fill with whatever you like. Every day you should strive to write something new in here, even if I do not explicitly state it. Use your initiative and imagination.

Let's start by giving the notebook a name/title. Call it something positive and encouraging. Mine was called *Operation Fix Up*, but maybe yours could be called *I Am the Best in the World* or *Notebook of Invincibility* or even *Dave Grohl.* Write this title on the cover or the first page. Then on the next page, I want you to write *DAY 01* at the top and then draw a smiley face beneath it. This may feel stupid but just do it. Draw a smiley face. Stop asking questions. I can't hear you.

Did you do that? Only you know. And on that note, I would like to take a moment to inform you that I'm not ignorant. I have read countless self-improvement books in my life, and my participation in each one was hugely varied. At times, I'd watch as a mental resistance would stack bricks into my core, and I'd downright refuse to follow the suggestions presented. How dare a book tell me what to do, right?

The simple fact of the matter is that I can't tell you what to do, nor can I even have any idea of whether or not you do anything whatsoever. I may have some killer advice for you here, but in the end, you hold all the strength. You hold me too, for I am but a book. You could set me on fire at any given point if you so wished, and how do you think that makes me feel? I am at your total mercy.

But let's level with one another for a second. The last thing in the world I want is for any of this feel like a school assignment because I know how unenergetic and uninspired these times of heartbreak can be. Believe me, I definitely definitely know. Which is why I will say this once and once only: do what you want. If you don't get the notebook, then you don't get the notebook. If you get the notebook but disagree with some of the things I propose you write down, then go off in your own direction, and interpret it in any manner you feel fit. For, just like your life and your problems, this is all yours, every bit of it. Approach it however you feel comfortable. But I assure you that what you put in, just like everything, is what you will get out. At the end of the day, it exclusively depends on how badly you want this pain to go away. And any dedication will be greatly rewarded. That is a promise.

"You'll always miss 100% of the shots you don't take."
— Wayne Gretzky

Ok, so now that we've got that out of the way, let's give it a go. Turn to the page, and at the top of it, write *DAY 02: MY GOALS FOR THE*

NEXT 30 DAYS. And then, do just that. Try to write down at least five goals you wish to achieve throughout this book, but also feel free to add to this list whenever the fancy strikes you throughout the upcoming month. It's true that we are calling each chapter a "day", but these are more like steps, and you can go back to anyone of them at any time to update or improve on it as you find the inspiration to do so. Once again, do not treat this as a homework exercise. Treat this as a fun summoning of power.

Examples may include:

- "I will not contact so-and-so"
- "I want to go on at least one date"
- "I won't kiss another person until I am ready"
- "I will follow this book every day"
- "I will not check whatstheirname's Facebook or when they were last online"
- "I will make plans to hang out at least four friends on four separate occasions"
- "I will fill my room with flowers"
- "I will cook at least two meals for my housemate/a friend"
- "I will keep my pubic hair neatly trimmed"
- "I will go on a solo outing once a week, maybe to the cinema or a walk in a park"

Please note: I have not mentioned anyone by name, and this was intentional. It's not because I don't know the name of the person who has hurt you (even though I don't). It's because you should avoid writing their name down in your holy notebook, as this is your special place. Call them something else, give them a nickname to create a distance, or even turn them into a character. How about referring to them as something like *Dust Mouse* or *Voldemort* or *So-And-So*? Something amusing, you know? Rename them as a non-threatening entity. Refer to them as so (privately!) from now on, reducing their weight even in your thought.

"Use your mind to think about things, rather than think of them. You want to be adding value as you think about projects and people, not simply reminding yourself they exist." — David Allen , Getting Things Done: The Art of Stress-Free Productivity

Back to your goals! Now, while it's always much more beneficial to be creative and come up with a personal list to reflect your circumstances, don't worry if you only repeat my previous examples for now. I chose those specific points because we will be looking at achieving them during this book anyway, so they are an excellent place to start, and you can come up with better custom ones as we go. No pressure at all, ever.

At the same time, don't worry if your goals seem a little ridiculous or even unrealistic. That's not the point of this exercise either. What matters is that you are making steady and conscious decisions to move forward, even if you don't necessarily believe you can do that just yet. It's about developing commitments. Cementing intentions. And by taking baby steps every day while documenting your progress in this special diary, together we can face forwards and use this list to focus on exactly where we want to go. And then it becomes a project. It becomes a game. It can even become… enjoyable? Hey, did you ever wonder how the idea for this very book started? Right here, baby!

And that, ladies and gentlemen, is this entire journey in a nutshell. It's to do something every single day to progress towards these goals. Even if this seems unfathomable right now, do not fear, because that's why I am here. It is my sole duty to load you with new ideas to help you edge along every single day, and this is all you need to remember. Remember to trust me. We got this.

"The journey of a thousand miles must begin with a single step."
— Lao Tsu

Before we say goodbye to the day, I just want to emphasise once more that this is a game, and like all good games, there will be obstacles, setbacks, and final bosses. Do not fool yourself; this is going to be a bumpy ride. You will find yourself fondly remembering the good times and forgetting the bad. You will crave the familiarity of simpler days. You will wonder what you could have done differently. You'll have fleeting moments when you secretly want to win this person back. Your ex may text you. You might hear your song on the radio. You might find out about a fun party they attended. Now and then, you'll want to break down like Day 1, and in those moments, let it happen. Designate some time to push out those emotions as hard and as often as they come, and then take a deep breath, marching forward with my words. Some days are going to suck really badly, it is inescapable. But this is an integral part of the healing process. And with this book, you will slowly learn how to deal with these tripwires without anyone even noticing.

I like to think of this book not as one of "lessons" but one of "lessens". Slowly but surely, we are going to loosen the ropes around your chest, and you will breath easier and easier as we go on. But for now, all you have to do is make this recovery period your priority. If you can avoid it, do not make any other drastic changes to your life, and place all of your attention into fixing this issue first and foremost. Do not move house (unless you live with your ex) or change jobs (unless you work with your ex) if you can. Today is not an ideal time to quit smoking or to get married to someone else. And just remember that people have climbed Mount Everest and beaten cancer before. If they can do that, then you can win this common fight to rediscover the person you once were, instead of a human who is missing half of themselves. A full person, all on their own, in 28 days from now.

"Anything in life worth having is worth working for."
— Andrew Carnegie

And so to recap...

Today, the game started. Your first mission: getting a notepad and writing down some goals, any goals at all, no matter how impossible or insignificant they may seem. By taking this one step, you have already started the journey towards your ultimate freedom.

Day 3
Moving Up The Emotional Ladder

Day 3
Moving Up The Emotional Ladder

"Faith is taking the first step even when you don't see the whole staircase." — Martin Luther King, Jr.

Today we will continue with the trend of taking things slowly, because how do you eat an elephant? One bite at a time. Have you heard that joke before? I like it. Don't eat an elephant, though.

By now most of us are well acquainted with the Kübler-Ross model, but for those who aren't, here is a brief summary:

Once upon a time, a bright Swiss psychiatrist named Elisabeth Kübler-Ross observed that there were five stages that her terminally ill patients typically went through when facing their mortality. This model was so impressive that it is now considered applicable to other processes of emotional development, such as substance abuse, a child's view on divorce, and of course, breakups. Below is a list of those stages complete with examples, so that you can locate which one applies to how you've been feeling the most of lately.

Denial: "Surely this is not the end. I'm fine with whatever either way."
Anger: "How dare they do this to me! This is all their fault!"
Bargaining: "Maybe if I call them and say the right thing, I can fix this? I can change. We can work this out."
Depression: "I am legit going to die without this person."
Acceptance: "This is over, and I need to move on."

"The five stages - denial, anger, bargaining, depression, and acceptance - are a part of the framework that makes up our learning to live with the one we lost. They are tools to help us frame and identify what we may be feeling. But they are not stops on some linear timeline in grief." — Elisabeth Kubler-Ross

This widely utilised system has remained popular for nearly four decades, but I find it a bit too simplified for the complexities of every emotional recovery. Which is why I took it upon myself to adapt and stretch out this Emotional Ladder just for you (inspired by the incredible works of Abraham Hicks, look it up!), specifying each rung a little further and, as a result, making them even more reachable. And it goes a little something like this:

The Emotional Ladder *(in descending order)*
1. Liberation!
2. Hopefulness and Excitement
3. Relief and Satisfaction
4. Boredom
5. Lost Confusion
6. Irritation, Frustration, and Impatience
7. Sadness, Loneliness, and Longing
8. Doubtfulness and Discouragement
9. Furious Anger
10. Vengeful Hatred
11. Destructive Hatred
12. Jealousy
13. Fearful Anxiety
14. Unlovable Worthlessness
15. Utter Devastation and Depression

"Strength and growth come only through continuous effort and struggle." — Napoleon Hill

The objective of such a list is to illustrate how impossible the gigantic leap from devastation is to liberation. You can't move from feeling terrible to feeling ok with a wink, because there are far too many emotions on the spectrum between them. It does not work that way.

Instead, study the ladder. Look over these options carefully and try to pinpoint the one which best describes how you are feeling right now, or recently in general. Got it? Ok good. Now write down that number and the associated emotion in your notebook for Day 3.

Now, look at the point directly above it. Write its name and number above the previous line you wrote. And then look at it. That is where you want to climb. That is your goal emotion right now. Your mission is to get from your current feeling and jump up one point on the list.

How to achieve this might require some imagination, but in theory, it shouldn't be too difficult. Turn your jealousy for someone into an external hatred for the world instead. Turn your desire of destruction into a more cunning plan of revenge. Turn your frustration into the bewildering question of why this has happened? And what is the meaning of life anyway? Certainly, you will still be in a place that no one wants to be, but the idea is that you are climbing a ladder towards eventual freedom, one rung at a time. Hell, you might even find this process so effortless, that you could attempt to climb even higher than just one step…

"Strength does not come from physical capacity. It comes from an indomitable will." — Mahatma Gandhi

Please do note, however, that this exercise is less about action and more about training your thoughts to function in a certain way (automatically seeking out an emotional shift). Don't actually inflict revenge on someone, otherwise I might get into trouble.

Throughout every day for the foreseeable future, you will inevitably experience an array of these emotions in any seemingly random order. The trick is to become aware of those suffering moments, and once you recognise (and can name) this negative energy dragging down your guts, come back to this list, and try to climb a little way upwards. It will take practice to build said awareness, but do not worry, for, during this entire book, I will be gently prodding you to revisit the concept.

Even if this day seems utterly nonsensical to you, it is still an important premise which illustrates heartbreak as a gradual process of recovery. No one is asking you to try and pretend that you are suddenly doing fine and are "over it", because that is the slap of denial all over your face. Rather, feel the pain, refuse to ignore it, and then tackle it straight-up, attempting to morph it into the next most logical emotion. And eventually... *eventually...* you will find yourself tapping on the realms of satisfaction, of excitement, and ultimately, of complete freedom. Take notice of this internal war, find a firmer grip, and then steadily beat the living daylights out of it.

"That which does not kill us makes us stronger." — Friedrich Nietzsche

And so to recap...

It won't be an instant wake-up call, but the idea here is to keep an eye on your emotions until you catch them in the act and can label them accordingly. Remember to use the Emotional Ladder whenever your feelings run away from you, and take note of what you discover along the way. There is nothing too small to be written down!

Day 4
Get It All Out

Day 4
Get It All Out

"You would think it best to save your breath for running, but I often find screaming helps." — Mark Lawrence

Today will be similar to Day 1, except instead of falling into ourselves, we're going to force all of that energy outwards. It may be fun. You may even enjoy it.

Do you know what the word *catharsis* means? It is defined as *"the process of releasing, and thereby providing relief from, strong or repressed emotions."* Which sounds pretty constructive when you look at it like that, right?

In my experience, one of the hardest aspects of a breakup is that you find yourself with an endless stream of questions and pent-up anger. These disturbances can compel us to perpetually contact the ex to upset them or to guilt-trip them into changing their mind or to uncover some closure that they will never be able to give to us. The even bigger problem here is that it often results in the opposite desired effect. We look pathetic, and we drive the other person even further away.

"Go on, get out! Last words are for fools who haven't said enough!" — Karl Marx

Now, I have to be general here. I have no idea what your specific situation entails, but whether someone has done you wrong, or if you think you've messed up, or if the mutual split has left you feeling as though your body has been sliced down the middle, none of this matters. What matters, is that you have a million thoughts and emotions scattered all over your insides right now, and we need to get them out, pronto.

There are many pathways one can take to achieve this, but they all start from the same place. So pick up your notepad and start writing, Day 04. Here you will be dumping all of your poisoned guts onto paper, away from your chest, out of your head, except with one little additional instruction. In this version, you have done no wrong.

Truthfully, nothing is ever black and white in this world. There will always be a spectrum of greys, two sides to every story, and there are very few examples when only one person is at fault when it comes to a breakup. Even when people cheat, they cheat because something else was wrong. There are bound to be multiple reasons why your relationship eventually imploded, and some of them will be because of you. But today, in our fantasy land, this is not the case. Today, you are the hero, and there is only one side to this story. Your side.

"When we don't know who to hate, we hate ourselves." — Chuck Palahniuk, Invisible Monsters

What's more, don't be polite about this. Be as scathing as you possibly can. Do not say a single negative thing about yourself, and place the entire blame on the other person, lit up by the fires from Hell. Whatever the reasons for your split, write down precisely what they did wrong because (even if this isn't the case) today is the day when it was them who ruined what you had. Anything you can think of which made them an undesirable partner; that made you angry; the stupid things they did which you couldn't stand; and how they ultimately destroyed the relationship… all of this needs to be written down, decorated by the most colourful language you can uncover from the sharpest pits of your vocabulary. Feel free to exaggerate if you like; no one is going to know. This is just a harmless exercise, no matter how ugly, and it will make sense as the days go on.

And so, recall the bad times.
Write down the worst memories.
Remember when they said that thing which was really hurtful?

And that time they embarrassed you in front of other people?
What part of their body did you like the least?
Did their breath smell funny in the morning?
What general habits and political/artistic opinions did you disagree with?
What annoying friend did they have?
What parts of your life did they not understand?
How have they messed you up?
How could have they tried harder?

The idea here is to pinpoint the details where the two of you didn't gel, and ultimately, did not work for whatever reason. Take your time. Think about what would have happened if the relationship didn't end. These troubles would still be an issue and would have only spiralled further. How bad could have things got? Imagine the worst. If this exercise hurts you and makes you furious, then you are doing it right.

"If you prick us do we not bleed? If you tickle us do we not laugh? If you poison us do we not die? And if you wrong us shall we not revenge?" — William Shakespeare, The Merchant of Venice

For additional points, why not get creative with this task? Some suggestions:

Write a terrible poem built up from these reflections, using expressive adjectives to tie the rhythm together, coming up with clever rhyming schemes about how you have been treated wrong.

Draw a comic book featuring characters based on your liking, illustrating your ex's faults as a villain, and your brilliance as the superhero who always comes out on top.

Write an emotional acoustic song in the voice of your favourite artist, pouring your hardships into the melody, singing as loud as you can through the tears, making up for any lack of talent with a zest of passion.

Paint a picture of the scene where they hurt you the most, except replace them with a monster and replace yourself as a cute little creature, unfairly treated.

Or just scribble a bunch of these memories all over a photo of them, whatever you like.

"Forgive me, but what is the purpose of drama but catharsis?"
— Edward Zwick

There is one small yet dangerous aspect to all of this. What might happen is that you could become very proud of these words which you've put down. Your self-confidence may rise, and you may marvel over your articulated feelings, perhaps finally reaching a breakthrough where you believe you know exactly what you want to say. If you went down the more artistic route, you might want to send your ex your sketched masterpiece of them hanging by a noose or upload a YouTube video of that song you wrote where you compared them to a sewer rat. In cases of this compulsion, this is what you do:

YOU DO NOT DO THAT.

There are two solid reasons why you must never entertain this thought.

REASON #1: Any such spontaneous action lacks the necessary analysis behind the consequences. I implore you, exercise patience, as the following two days will be directly dealing with these exact topics. A tiny slice of self-control is all I'm asking for here. Get through tomorrow and the next day, and if you still feel the need to unleash these thoughts onto your ex and the world, then I won't try and stop you. However, you should also carefully consider this…

REASON #2: You still have work to do. Do you really think you can get all of your thoughts and emotions out in one day? Especially when we have so many chapters ahead of us? We are going to uncover an array of other assorted feelings and ideas, delving deep into the dunes of your heartbreak. Why would you hastily blow your full power prematurely? Wouldn't you rather build a proper case before unveiling your concluding statement? Because we are going to do just that, very soon.

"Self-respect is the root of discipline: The sense of dignity grows with the ability to say no to oneself." — Abraham Joshua Heschel

And that's what makes today a special day. Every time you feel the yearning of them returning, here is the day to come back to, reading over what you wrote in your notepad to remind you of how they mistreated your aching heart. Every time you remember something new they did wrong, or something upsetting about their character, come back to this page and add to the list, finding creative ways of expressing these emotions accordingly. Do not let these venomous words dwell in your mind. Let those toxins drips from your pen with all the agony you can muster, expressed in any which way you can flex your creative juices, and then leave them here.

I want to end today with an important elaboration on an earlier point. I am sure some of you may find today's exorcism leads to feelings of great distress, where you ponder about unresolved questions, confused by recent decisions, desiring certain clarifications. This is to be expected. This will happen again. And even if this was not your experience today, it is still bound to occur more than once during the pages ahead.

Treat this just as **REASON #2** stated above. Do not rush to your phone every time curiosity nags, convincing you that you've finally found the right words you've been seeking. This won't be the case. A new question will present itself as soon as you blurt the last one out, every time.

Instead, turn to your back page, and start to note down any questions for your ex that you still don't understand. Throughout this book, allow that list of queries to build up. By the time you've reached a state of clear-headedness and are not acting on impulse, you will have accumulated an impressive collection of these inquiries. Develop some patience and deal with these issues later, all at once. Stay tuned, and together we will work out when this ideal moment is well-cooked and ready to be unleashed.

"One's dignity may be assaulted, vandalised and cruelly mocked, but it can never be taken away unless it is surrendered."
— Michael J. Fox

And so to recap...

Today was the day to conjure as many nasty thoughts as possible then shove them somewhere external (as in, your notebook). The idea is to move information from your head and into a different realm. This is to clear your mind and give you an outlet to add new content to whenever some other troublesome thought comes up.
We will use this later, hence why you should only attempt this if you have enough willpower not to send the results to your anyone, especially your ex! Be strong! You'll find out why soon.

Day 5
Cut Them Off

Day 5
Cut Them Off

"Because at some point you have to realise that some people can stay in your heart but not in your life." — Sandi Lynn

One long chapter coming up, and I apologise for it, but if you follow my words, then by the end of today, your life will be different.

Now that we've spent the last few days dealing with our insides, it is time to turn our efforts around and start making outside actions. Here is where things get a touch more uncomfortable and scary, but do not worry, I am still around.

First and foremost, let's address the virtual world as a natural approach to the topic—in particular, social media. These platforms are a recent development in our current society, something our ancestors did not have to think about when it came to breaking up. In our lives, however, these useful tools can turn against us during these dismal periods, shoving everyone else's business into your face, and your business into everyone else's face. These have benefits in our everyday lives, but in the turmoil of breakups, they tend to leave a mess.

"It's a highly deceptive world, one that constantly asks you to comment but doesn't really care what you have to say."
— David Levithan, Two Boys Kissing

There is a good chance you've already independently addressed this facet in your process, but if you haven't, or even if you have, I recommend you read through these following points very carefully and evaluate your circumstances with them in mind.

As far as I can see (and I wear contact lenses), you have four options to consider when it comes to handling your online presence in conjunction to your ex, each of which has their own unique set of pros and cons. Like so:

Option 1: Do Nothing

This approach is when you keep your ex on your Friends/Follow lists, and it is the option I recommend the least. By holding these avenues open, you remain involved with their every move, as their existence incessantly scrapes at the crevices of your brain, reminding you that they are still here. Even worse, it makes it oh-so-easy to spy on them, stalk them, or send them a message in a weaker moment. Of course, you are you, and if you honestly feel the most torturous path is the best choice for you, then I am not going to argue. However, please do keep reading with an open mind, and let's see if I can talk some sense into you.

"I think the very word stalking implies that you're not supposed to like it. Otherwise, it would be called 'fluffy harmless observation time'." — Molly Harper

Option 2: The Ninja Approach

This was my preferred weapon of choice. I simply hid them from my newsfeeds, gone, and unfollowed them on Instagram and Twitter and whatever other things the kids use these days. They may eventually notice your absence, but it will probably take them a while, and that's not the point. You should even go deeper than this, and (as tough as this may be) archive their conversations on Whatsapp and Gtalk or wherever you used to chat, and if they spring up again, archive it all once more. You want to minimise the chances of their name crossing your eyes at every turn possible.

The reason why I favoured this practice above the others is purely down to the evil in me. I wanted them to see my social media updates (and I will elaborate more on that tomorrow) because this meant that they were perpetually reminded of me, whilst I wasn't bombarded with their rubbish every day. I never said I was a saint.

This option does come with additional risk, however. The curiosity will eat you alive. You will forever feel the overwhelming compulsion to check their social profiles or see when they were last online. You will probably give in and do this a few times because God knows I did. But if this urge suddenly grabs you and you find yourself typing their name into the search bar, use all of your strength to ask yourself the following question: *am I ready to make myself feel miserable again?* Because that is all you will achieve.

Just viewing one photo of them having fun or witnessing an attractive stranger writing on their wall or literally anything at all... these are the things that can completely mess up your day. No matter what you see, you will think the worst and take everything out of context, pulling your entire healing process backwards.

Keep in mind that curiosity may be an uncomfortable sensation, but it always feels so much better than the confirmation of fears. And every time you manage to defeat this impulse, take note of it in your diary or reward yourself in some proud way because that is a massive achievement. Alternatively, if you find you are unable to control your stalk time whatsoever, think about upgrading your option to one of these next ones:

Option 3: Cut Them Off Completely

Taking things up a notch would be the deletion/unfollowing of them on every other platform, erasing their number from your phone, ripping their page out of your phonebook, etc etc.

It's a tough decision to make, but you will reap massive benefits. Even if you fall victim to your stalking yearning, your viewing permissions will now be limited depending on their privacy settings. As frustrating as this may feel in times of obsessive inquisitiveness, it will protect you from harm in the long run. Furthermore, keep in mind that this works as a double punch, as it sends the silent message to your ex that you are no longer willing to dedicate time to their thoughts and have banished them from your screens. It's more challenging to go back from that in your moments of weakness. Furthermore, there should be a great sense of liberation following this choice, and it might be the exact declaration of independence you need right now.

"Life is too short to hold grudges, true, but cutting people off for self-preservation isn't a grudge, it's applying wisdom." — Unknown

Option 4: Severe Their Head Right Off

Not literally, but you can go to extreme levels if you are that deep within the hole of upset. As follows: block them on every platform you have. Block their phone number, their emails, their messages, their chats, their usernames. Do everything in your power to burn all avenues of communication just short of opening a restraining order. If you have the guts for this, then I fully have your back. They will be properly gone, and you will move forward at a much faster rate because you won't even be able to look back if you wanted to. There won't be anything to look back on, because you erased it all.

"Empty packets of hot sauce remind me of the love I used to have for her. Now all I'm left with is this yummy taco. " — Jarod Kintz, A Zebra is the Piano of the Animal Kingdom

Ok, so that's done! Great! But of course, the virtual world is not the end-all answer, as we have that pesky physical life to take care of too. And it goes without saying that you must avoid them at all costs. I know this isn't always easy, for in many cases, a masochistic part of your heart really really wants to see them. This is because, as we discussed on Day 1, you are essentially a drug addict having withdrawal symptoms. But just like you can't quit cigarettes by smoking cigarettes, and just like you can't quit cocaine by doing lines of cocaine, that one more hit is not going to do anything except exasperate the issue. It's ridiculous when you put it like that, so just remember why you picked up this book in the first place: to move on. Which is why, if there is a social gathering, and they are going, *DO NOT GO.* It will hurt to stay at home and feel sorry for yourself, but do you know what will hurt more and for longer? Seeing their face.

For certain scenarios, however, this is a little easier said than done. Perhaps you keep finding yourself sleeping with this person. Perhaps you work together. Perhaps you live together. Perhaps you are married. Perhaps you even have children together. These circumstances need to be treated more carefully, and there is no easy way around it. All I can suggest is following the same procedure as already illustrated. Avoid them in any way you can. Get a new job if it's too painful. Speak to your boss about shuffling things around if they can. Stay with a family member or a friend until you can find a new place to live. Do absolutely anything you can think of without making excuses. Create a distance between the two of you, otherwise this is going to take an extremely long time to heal (if it ever heals at all). Keep on reading, and we'll come back to this before the chapter is over.

Oh, but please, if this applies to you, then stop having sex with them right now! This is like injecting cookie dough into your veins. It may clog up your broken heart arteries for a brief time, but once that dissolves, your sugar cravings will have only escalated, and your heart will be an even bigger wreck. There are very few suggestions that every guide I've read about breaking up agree upon, but this is one of them. The sun will come up, and life will be worse than before. Break this habit.

"To save face, it's better not to ask sex from the ex, but to give everything the axe." — Anthony Liccione

There is always the chance that none of this applies because they've already made the decision for you. Perhaps you've been cut off from *their* social media, and perhaps they are avoiding *you* at all costs. I make no joke about the pain this must have caused, but on the flip side, there is a fantastic advantage to this position. The ex has made the *no contact* call before you. The hardest choice is out of your hands, and all you have to do is deal with it. There's less for you to think about, so just march away. And this is how you do that:

You must start by getting rid of everything that puts their face into your thoughts. Tall order? Sure. But if you're serious about moving on, then please note that there will be no greater freedom than deleting all of their emails, all of your online conversations, all of your phone messaging, everything, gone. Remove all the songs that remind you of them from your playlist. Throw away their cosmetics, their toothbrush, whatever they kept at your house. Untag or even delete all the lovey-dovey photos of you together on social media. Throw away (or burn!) every love letter and gift they have ever given you, eradicating their presence from your house like an insect blasted with bug spray. If this feels too drastic to you, I understand, but at very least put that stuff in a box and put that box in the attic. Perhaps even download your photos and conversations (without reading them!) then slap them on a USB drive before erasing them. In that way, these could be fun relics you accidentally discover when you're older, laughing hysterically at how this silly person made you feel so horrible all that time ago. But for now, clear the path to happiness by removing every painful obstacle, out of reach, out of existence.

"When we are in love, we are convinced nobody else will do. But as time goes, others do do, and often do do, much much better."
— Coco J. Ginger

For some of you, this day of ceremonial purifications will fill you with a newfound abundance of strength, but for others, you may feel even worse. What if you still really want to be this person's friend? What if you are secretly hoping that one you can work this all out? What if you enjoy your communication, it's special to you, and you don't want to lose that? Well, I am going to play psychic here, and presume that you've already tried this? And it's not exactly helping?

Your mental health is under strain because of how you've been holding on? Hence why you picked up this book, maybe? But that's not the point either, is it?

I extend the following advice to those cases: if this person truly is worth something to you, and you don't envision their brutal death, then use today to tell them what you are doing. Explain to them that you need to take a month away from them, to cool off, and to collect your thoughts. A month will reveal the right answers to you without picking at the scabs, and once it's over, you will be in a much healthier place to address the issue. If they are deserving of an eventual friendship, then they will understand this period of non-communication. If they do not understand this, then they deserve nothing. Be open, and give this book your best shot. It's only one month.

And truth be told, depending on the situation, a month could be far too short of a time to cut contact anyway. In the vast majority of circumstances, my recommendation is that you should only see this person once you don't even want to see them anymore. And in all fairness, for as long as you are reading this book, you are probably not ready, so don't rush this part of the process because very few things can flick your dominoes faster than the premature invitation of an ex's hand.

"The best way to move forward is to let go of the people holding you back." — Unknown

And thus ends all of your contact with this individual, *ta-da*, well done. Of course, this doesn't stop them from sending *you* a message, and then the game levels-up, expert mode. If they do send you a text or an email, the best-case scenario is not to read it. Still, a decent case scenario is to read it but not respond. However, there will be those other scenarios when you have to answer, and your response is unavoidable (for example if you have kids or a mortgage together). In this case, do not fear. Take note of very this page in your notebook right now, and come running back here in these situations, following this list, step by step:

1. Unless it's an emergency, always wait at least an hour before responding. This will give you time to calm down, to articulate your thoughts, and prioritise your mind over your emotions, while also making you look anything but desperate/angry/intense/whatever.

2. Keep your response polite and peaceful. Never respond in fury or pain. Respond only from a position of courteous neutral apathy, even if you fake it.

3. Keep your responses as concise as possible. The fewer words you use, the better. Deal with the business at hand but do not entertain anything else. Do not bring up any other topic of conversation. Do not attempt to be smart by hiding sneaky subtexts or snide in-jokes between the lines. This is not clever. It will only open a crack which taunts them to climb through. One-worded replies are for the true masters of the game. If the ex veers off-topic, stop responding. If they invite you out, casually decline, or even better, stop responding.

4. *NEVER* leave the message open for further conversation. Make your statement without the invitation to keep the ball rolling. If your message contains a single question mark, you are probably doing it wrong. If they respond anyway, follow this list over, keeping in mind that no reply is still your strongest reply.

"Never miss a good chance to shut up." — *Will Rogers*

I am going to repeat that: *no reply is still your strongest reply.* If they are begging for you to come back or have become insulting or demanding, simply by offering a response, you have unlocked the gates of discussion, which is the complete opposite of what you want here. Where will it end? Each response will prompt another response, every time you will only have more things to say, and it will go on forever. You need to create space.

If they phone you, never pick up, because no matter how strong you feel, you can never trust the first thoughts out of your mouth when you have a broken heart. It can spiral too quickly. They will leave a voice message or text you if it's urgent. If contact is necessary, keep it written never spoken. Grant your dignity the space to construct a draft, edit, undo, start again. You will sound far more articulate and levelheaded that way.

Something you may have realised by now is that a lot of this game is actually against yourself. You will forever question if you did the right thing by skipping that call. You will wonder what it was they meant by that cryptic message. You will yearn for their thoughts on your feelings. But trust me on this, if they give you that information, your brain will flood with a whole new batch of traumatic emotions, and this will knock you way backwards. The fresher the speculations you develop on the matter, the harder it will be to reign them in.

As far as today is concerned, this is what you need to remember: you are here to get over this person. You will never get to say everything you want to say because there will always be more stuff to say. You have already said enough. So put those thoughts, and those memories, and that person, away. And let's move forward.

*"You can spend minutes, hours, days, weeks, or even months over-analysing a situation; trying to put the pieces together, justifying what could've, would've happened... or you can just leave the pieces on the floor and move the f**k on." — Tupac Shakur*

And so to recap...

Today was the incredibly difficult but highly important day where you looked over your options about removing your ex from your life.
It was a long chapter, but you must consider the information carefully. The decisions you make now will affect the rest of our journey immensely. Whenever you're ready, write down what you have decided to do, and stick to it.

Day 6
Dealing With Everyone Else

Day 6
Dealing With Everyone Else

"Oftentimes, when people are miserable, they will want to make other people miserable too. But it never helps." — Lemony Snicket, The Blank Book

Yesterday, we looked at the connection between you and that one other individual. Today, we will be looking at this same connection, except with everyone else in mind.

Now, as is human nature, you are probably currently harbouring a strong urge to publicise your self-pity. You want people to know that you are hurt, and you'd prefer those people take your side rather than your ex's side. The good news is that achieving this outcome is easy. But the bad news is that it's also the fastest way to disgrace your face.

"If you can't say something nice, don't say nothing at all." — Thumper's Law

You must keep in mind that no matter how hard done by you may feel at this time, often the most unfairly treated casualties of a breakup are the mutual friends. Which is why you should always refrain from slagging your ex off to them, and instead request that these individuals keep their positions neutral. This isn't straightforward and isn't what comes naturally, but there are powerful reasons for doing so.

The main reason is that it grants you more control over the situation, even if it doesn't initially feel like it. By rising above the issue without any demands and openly recognising the group of friends' awkward position, these people will undoubtedly appreciate your mature outlook. They will be relieved that you are not pulling them into the mess (of which they have very little do with). It will be liberating for all of you, and yet is not the only asset you will gain.

Imagine your ex is demanding these mutual friends pick sides, whilst you are the one asking them not to. Whose team are they most likely to take?

Regardless, when it comes to mutual people who are closer to your ex than you, I would suggest that you *don't* delete them from your life if you can, otherwise, they will turn on you. Rather mute all of their accounts, as so to avoid tagged photos and constant reminders.

On another critical side note, if you have kids: *Leave. Them. Out. Of. It.* No excuses. They are like next-level mutual friends, and this is harder for them than it is for you. Speak no ill of the other parent in their presence, or you may cause unseen damage that lasts a lifetime.

"Misery loves company, but company does not reciprocate."
— Addison Mizner

Moving on and going back to the social media conversation, it is so easy these days to have a public meltdown with the click of a button. We need to try our best to avoid this occurrence. Of all the solutions, there would be no healthier suggestion than getting off of these platforms altogether. Take a break from the digital world and unplug from the bombardment of useless information about other people's gym routines and food porn. Focus on your life for a while. I have friends who took themselves off the grid, never to return, and are much happier for it. If you are this way inclined, give it a go, as it is inarguably your most excellent move in this circumstance. But for certain people (such as myself), internet restraint is far beyond our capabilities, and we need a more practical guide to help us present a friendlier version of ourselves even when that's not how we feel. Hello, this is that guide.

As before, mutual friends may want the best for you, but if you're continually announcing how the ex has done you wrong or how miserably low you are, it's going to start to put their emotional investment in a strange place. They may eventually retreat their dedication to your cause because this is not their fight. Beyond this, please note that there may be someone following your account right now who is your perfect match. They could have a big crush on you, ready to make the final move, but upon seeing how dark your vibe has become as well as the hatred you can spew, they might feel repulsed and turn away. Don't let either of these things happen.

"Mixing humour and harsh reality is a very human behaviour, it's the way people stay sane in their daily lives." — Jorge Garcia

Instead, emphasise every sliver of positivity that you can whenever you feel the urge to post your feelings online, or at very least spin it into something humorously dark (which is what I did). Such actions will not only help you feel like your head is above the death line but even more so, will give others the impression that you are constructively dealing with your emotions. And when your ex asks the mutual friends how you are doing, they will report that you're doing well, and the ex won't like hearing that. Perhaps this isn't the ideal reasoning for doing so, but what is the alternative? Displaying your depression for all the world to see? That will only bring you down, and bring everyone else around you down too. Even worse, it will turn into a self-fulfilling prophecy. If you repeat that this breakup is the worst thing ever, then it will become the worst thing ever. If you tell people that, yes, it sucks, but you are taking the necessary steps to sort it out, your mental headspace will listen and obey. That's how the brain works. It's trainable. You can lie to it until the lie becomes the truth. Plus, it's your brain, so there's no moral obligation to be truthful anyway.

"The best way to mend a broken heart is time and girlfriends."
— Gwyneth Paltrow

Of course, there is no value in slapping a happy sticker over your mouth and pretending everything is ok. No one is asking you to do that. What I'm asking you to do, is to refrain from setting off an atomic bomb of emo drama in the middle of your social circle, then forcing the shrapnel of your despair into the eyes of every single person you've ever met. Maintaining a public face of consideration is important, but at the same time, privately bouncing thoughts between friends is a healthy avenue too. Crawling into a hermit shell won't work. Seeking support in those who would seek support in you will work. Select a few special friends or family members who know you the best and vent to them, finding relief in the people who will help you carry this weight. However, even this therapeutic escape comes with its own set of unique caveats. If you are in a perpetual slump of bleakness, your draining presence will turn into a tedious bore, and soon enough, even your closest of friends will associate you with having a bad time. They may even begin to resent or avoid your company.

"What happens when people open their hearts? They get better."
— Haruki Murakami, Norwegian Wood

My rules to prevent myself from turning into an inconvenient nuisance were very simple. I'd spread my troubles over as many people as possible, meaning that no one human had to endure the full burden of my tears and feel solely responsible for the recovery. I achieved this by meeting a different friend at least once a week, a one-on-one basis type of conversation, where I'd cautiously unleash my woes and, in return, get a fresh perspective, different than the one before. In addition to this approach, I would never say the same thing to the same person twice, because what would be the point? There are only so many times someone can listen to the repetitive story of how so-and-so mistreated you, and there is absolutely no value in doing so. Where will it end?

Tell them what happened. Tell those friends how you feel. Make sure they understand your position. Be open to what you did wrong too. And then try to move the conversation forward into related realms that you have never covered before. Because that's how you utilise people for what they are: humans with unique brains who will make you feel better in their own way, helping you to explore new angles you'd never considered. What they are not, are emotional punching bags.

Try to follow the previous three paragraphs to the letter. Pick up the phone right now and organise your first friend-meet for this or the following week (if not in person, then video chat will suffice). Continue to do so for each week that passes, lining up a new set of ears on a seven-day turnover basis. That is your task for today. Organise to meet a friend within the next week, and continue to do so every week from then on. Take note of it.

"We have two ears and one mouth so that we can listen twice as much as we speak." — Epictetus

Finally, talking is the second most important aspect of this step. The most important aspect is, as you'd assumed, listening. Sometimes you will find your friends will turn the conversation around. Even though you are the one hurting, they will relate it to their past experience, perhaps by saying something like "*I remember when me and (x) broke up two years ago...*" or "*I know exactly what you are going through right now, it's like when I...*" etc.

"Listen to many, speak to a few." — William Shakespeare

These words may feel annoying and probably won't help, but go with it. Do not focus solely on yourself. Listen to their clichés and give them the time to speak. Most of their obscure rubbish will be utterly irrelevant to your life, but don't be rude about it. They are trying to help, their hearts are in the right place, and you never know when you may just strike gold. Because that's where your side of the friendship comes in. Take their advice and do whatever they tell you to. If they suggest you watch a particular movie about breakups which is guaranteed to make you cry, then do it. If they inform you of a comedy which would cheer you right up, go and watch it. If they speak about a self-help book which guided them through their tough times, go out and buy it. If they suggest a seminar in town, check it out. Ask them about their heartbreak experiences and methods. Get led to water, and drink. Chances are, you won't want to, and none of it will help in any way, but it works on a level much more significant than that. It is you taking action, which provides the sliver of hope you are chasing. Pick up the diary and write down what you did that day, noting each step you took, then move forward using the hands of others.

"Honesty is the first chapter of the book wisdom."
— Thomas Jefferson

Hey, you want to know what else can be fun? Unleash your emotional woes onto strangers. If the random person at the shop or your Uber driver asks you how you are, be honest and tell them. Give them the summary of your breakup and tell him how much you are hurting. You'll never see them again; they have no ties to the situation, they may feel awkward, but there are no casualties in your immediate social circle, and the release will do you good. Give that a try!

Hey, you want to know what can also be fun? Throw a party celebrating your newly found freedom! Invite only exceptional humans and get a whole load of friendship love at once! Cheers to the new you! Woohoo! Friends!

"Everybody will help you. Some people are very kind." — Bob Dylan, I'll Keep It With Mine

And so to recap...

Your mission for today is simple: pick up the phone and organise a plan to meet up with a friend within the next seven days. Make notes in your calendar to keep this up. A new set of ears, every week, no excuses.

And remember: use these social sessions not only to vent but to listen too, taking their advice very seriously no matter how unhelpful it may seem. It's better than nothing!

Day 7
Extending The Circle Of Help

Day 7
Extending The Circle Of Help

"Admitting that you need help doesn't make you broken. It makes you fixable. And teachable." — Anonymous

Hi! As we spoke about yesterday, your friends may be able to lend a much needed helping hand in your time of disarray, but these hands often come laced with the bias of some previous investment in your relationship. They have been covered by a sticky situation which they have to deal with themselves. Similarly, I am here to guide you, but I am only a book at the end of the day. Our conversations are very one-sided, as is the nature of books.

Hence why you should consider looking beyond these immediate options. Depending on your current level of desperation, there is no shame in seeking professional help. Now, if you're anything like me, then your core instinct flairs into defence mode at the very mention of the idea. Is therapy not the surrender of all power? The ultimate admission of hopelessness? No, as I found out, it is not.

On the contrary, it is often the bravest move someone can make. You can hang up your useless pride for a moment and seek a greater understanding by hiring an outside brain to construct larger weaponry. It will not only be advantageous to acquire an outlook from someone who is outside of the situation, but you must also remember that these are experts trained in dealing with your exact brand of turmoil.

"I've realised therapy is incredibly therapeutic." — Lisa Schroeder; I Heart You, You Haunt Me

I am going to be a little blunt right now, so put on your sturdiest hard hat and prepare yourself for the kicker. What you are currently going through is not special. It is one of the most well-documented causes of severe distress known to humankind. This idea may melt your snowflake, but it is imperative for you to hear, and even more vital for you to understand how brilliant this news is. It means there are proven techniques already developed to navigate you out of this pit, and what's more, there are people who know how to teach them to you. Simply put: no one goes to therapy and gets worse.

"I love therapy! There's nothing like talking to someone who has no emotional tie to your life." — Eva Mendes

Perhaps the value is simply having someone to chat with. In more extreme cases, maybe this means a medical prescription which could be the gentle prod to get you out of bed in the morning. Of course, one should always be careful with medication because dependencies can develop quickly, and then you'll have a brand new problem. That said, it may also provide you with the crutch which keeps you away from the noose and can prop you up until you can stand on your own. Many of us will take a tablet for a headache, so don't be too quick to reject anything.

"But the main thing is that medication, too, is not all the help." — Tanya Tucker

Of course, as with anything in this book, do not feel obliged to take this therapy route if you do not feel comfortable with it. But sometimes, it can be a relief just to know that there are an endless array of qualified brains which are more than willing to open themselves up to your issues. Mainly because they get paid for it. On that topic, if you can't afford to get this type of help or if there is a dangerously long waiting list, consider Googling emotional support groups in your area. They are often free, and by listening to other stories from troubled individuals, your turmoil could shrink within a higher perspective. It can also be very cleansing to have a designated period of your day where you are encouraged to feel as sorry for yourself as possible in front of an open audience. It's a difficult environment to find otherwise.

What this chapter means to you can be identified by asking yourself the following question: *Am I in serious mental trouble right now, and do I need help to get out of it?*

If you answered *no*, then that's ideal! Thank you for giving me the time to cover this essential subject for the benefit of others. Feel free to forget all about it, and we'll pick up your path again tomorrow.

However, if you answered *yes*, then spend today looking around, researching what options you have available to you. Call your doctor. See what local support groups exist. Speak to a close friend who you know has been through a similar process. Take this step to uncover the root of the problem, as this could very well be the most beneficial day for many of you. I know it fast-tracked my recovery. Immeasurably so.

Finally, if you're already attending some form of therapy sessions, then you're ahead of the curve on this thing. Five-stars!

"You can be as miserable or angry about anything as much as you want. At the end of the day getting emotional will not solve any of your problems. The only thing you can do is keep moving forward because whether or not you are ready, life will always go on with or without you." — Anonymous

And so to recap...

Today is about toying with the idea of therapy. Weigh up the pros and cons. Look at what's available in your area. Even if you aren't comfortable or if you already attend sessions, use this day to contemplate impartial, external help.

Day 8
Self Medication

Day 8
Self Medication

"The first thing in the human personality that dissolves in alcohol is dignity." — Unknown

Sure, the professionals can numb us with pills to make our lives tolerable, but what's the point when we can just do it ourselves, am I right?

Well, this depends on you, as does everything.

I know how it feels. There are fleeting visions of our ex having a wonderful time without us, laughing at how much we held them back whilst they mess around with multiple partners who are all far superior lovers than we ever were. Terrible thoughts. Painful. Wait, I have an idea! Let's drown those horrific feelings in floods of booze and bury them beneath mountains of drugs immediately! That should show them! Yay!

Of course, this is akin to shoving fistfuls of cotton wool into an open wound in hopes that it will stop the bleeding. It may work for a little while, but ultimately, you are going to end up with a severe infection, and you will die.

"People who drink to drown their sorrow should be told that sorrow knows how to swim." — Ann Landers

Alcohol has the notorious reputation of morphing into the devil. It whispers into your ear, giving you a million brand new things to get mad about, encouraging you to break something or jump off a bridge. Or, at very least, pass these nasty thoughts onto your ex as fast as possible. Why do you think the term "drunk-dialling" has integrated itself so abundantly into today's culture? It's because you suddenly have all the words in the world and you think you know exactly how to articulate them and you must let everyone know.

By now, you've probably experienced this phenomenon before. What's more, I'm willing to bet that, after sending those texts/posting those messages and going to bed, you woke up in a panic. You reread your previous writings only to find that your spelling would have failed fourth grade and all of your poetic gushings were not quite as eloquent as you had previously assumed. Plus, you're hungover, and you're alone, forced to deal with these distressing thoughts and a messy room. As if you weren't already at a low point in your life! What was that damn alcohol thinking?

"Drugs are a waste of time. They destroy your memory and your self-respect and everything that goes along with your self-esteem." — Kurt Cobain

The same goes for drugs, if you're that way inclined. You will go up, and the pain will be smudged, but then you will come crashing way down, dumped in a pit far worse than before, and you will crave those former arms of comfort due to a pain more excruciating than anything you've ever felt sober. It's like making a deal with a demon, allowing him to smack you in the face with a much larger club, just so long as he takes a small break before he does so. It makes no sense.

And so, here I come with my advice: if you can, take a hiatus from self-medication completely. If your lifestyle does not warrant for this type of self-control, then please at least cut it down as much as possible. Any clued up person will tell you that you need a clear head to best deal with your situation, and by attacking your system with toxins, you will only diminish your strength, of which you need as much as you can get. You will discover nothing but temporary illusions by playing with these cards, merely disorientating you further in the long run. You will never be able to solve nor heal these wounds in any environment other than that of a clean mind. If you were to ask your mommy, she would agree.

"Drink because you are happy, but never because you are miserable." — G.K. Chesterton, Heretics

But, wait, if we are supposed to be going out with our friends, isn't a cheeky drink or two simply part of the social obligations? For many of us, this is inescapably true. If this is your situation, then recognise the difference between getting drunk with friends once a week and obliterating your feelings every day alone.

Regardless, even these outings come with some risk, because at some point, the night will end, and it will be just you, your phone, and Satan on your shoulder, poking your eardrum with a fiery pitchfork. *"Text the ex!"* he will say. So what then?

Well, depending on how well you dealt with Day 5, this could all be a non-issue. If you have a reputation for these drunk mishaps, perhaps revisit that step and consider severing the ties with your ex a little more viciously, because then you don't even have the tokens to play. However, I can't tell you how to live your life. All I can provide is guidance, which is what I am about to do.

"Why did she do this? She was a terrible drunk texter. All the things she wanted to say to people during the day came out at night, like a vampire." — Harriet Evans, Happily Ever After

Do me a favour, and read the paragraph after this one very carefully. Then, if you would, reread it. Then again. Then write it out in your diary word for word. Then read it again, from your own handwriting. And again. I know you're not going to do this, but I hope my incessant drilling is at least hyping you up, emphasising how important this is. You need to save the following words into your brain as a file which will automatically pop up when you find yourself in that vulnerable drunken about-to-text-the-ex state. Are you ready to hear it? It goes like this:

If I, [insert your name here], feel the urge to text or call my ex when I am intoxicated, I will first start by writing my message down elsewhere. I will compose my thoughts externally, either on paper or on my phone as a note. I will rewrite and then edit these thoughts until they are absolutely perfect. And then I will put them away and go to sleep as soon as possible. They will still be there 24-hours later, after which time I can grant them one more check to iron out any embarrassing typos or-overly emotional dribble. If they are as brilliant as I thought they were whilst I was drunk then, and only then, do I give myself full permission to send that message.

Above is what I call *heavily suggested advice*. You should read this often. You should read it out loud before you even leave the house to go drinking. Get it tattooed on the back of your hand so you can slap yourself with it if you forget.

"I have this disease late at night sometimes, involving alcohol and the telephone." — Kurt Vonnegut, Slaughterhouse-Five

I guarantee you that if you manage this task, you will wake up in an all-encompassing self-appreciation that you did not spill your guts during a moment where you could hardly think. Because, if you had done so, your ex would've rightfully disregarded you like the drunk idiot you were. Meanwhile, you would have crawled up into the fetal position of shame, wishing there was a button to make your life disappear. But by using the above approach instead, something magical will take place. You will have explored that special dramatic fury/misery your intoxicated heart provided, and then you will have exorcised it into text, all written down, never lost. Even better, you have not yet released it into the world, and so it is yours, still in your control, and can be pruned into a neater, sharper object of pain. You can reread it, fix the inevitable grammatical errors, and then decide if you still want to send it when your brain is more functional. And should you even send it? ***NO.*** Remember our conversation on Day 5 and use your sober advantage to veto that decision at all costs. We're not supposed to be making any contact this month if you recall.

If you're serious about this recovery process (and you said you were!), then transfer those words into your diary, eat a greasy breakfast as a reward for taking control of the situation, and then promise yourself that you're never going to drink again for the millionth time.

"Always do sober what you said you'd do drunk. That will teach you to keep your mouth shut." — Ernest Hemingway

And so to recap...

Today was the obligatory cautionary against intoxicating the pain away with particular focus on the devil's drunk-dial. Spare some in-depth thought to limiting these destructive poisons, and make a note of the mantra provided to preempt any messaging temptations!

Day 9
Reevaluation Day

Day 9
Reevaluation Day

"If you truly want to be respected by people you love, you must prove to them that you can survive without them." — Michael Bassey Johnson, The Infinity Sign

Oh my Gosh, can you believe it's already been a week since we started taking this mission seriously on Day 2? Maybe you can, but whatever, I'm proud of you (as much as words on a page can be anyway).

Here's a new regular action: at weekly intervals, we will be pausing to reflect upon where we have come from and taking stock of where we currently are. Use these days wisely, noting when you have excelled and where you have weakened, then using this information to reapproach specific strategies from different angles. It's a valuable exercise, as important as any of the others, as it grants you a small window of breathing room while guaranteeing that no aspect of your recovery gets left behind. So let us begin.

"Life can only be understood backwards; but it must be lived forwards." — Søren Kierkegaard

Arguably the most valuable point thus far was the one dealing with the communication between you and your ex. Have you managed to hold this agreement with yourself and not make contact with the person? Or did you stumble at some point? Is it worth looking back at Day 5 and working out a new approach? Or are you nailing this part of the process? Whatever is going on, don't beat yourself up about this, because it's reevaluation day! And we must never be hard on ourselves on reevaluation day! Rather, write down in your diary how this last week has been going in that regard, and make alterations to your former strategy if needs be. What haven't you tried? What triggered your most recent hiccup?

Another crucial topic we addressed would be that of friends and the public broadcasting of your emotional state. Have you managed to keep it together, at least out loud? Or have you been uncontrollably vomiting your emotions all over the place for the whole world to see? Remember that doing so only makes you look feeble, and even if it may provide some of the mass sympathy belly-rubs you are aching for right now, I guarantee you that a large percentage of your listeners have grown tired of hearing it. As annoying as this is, people have their own lives to deal with, and the more we beg them to care about ours, the less they will. That said (and as we already covered), venting is an essential part of healing, so I hope you have also been exploring one-on-one chats with people who you can trust. You should have already met up with (or made a plan meet up with) at least one person by now. If you haven't, welcome to your daily task.

Have you been watching your drinking and other toxin levels? Have you thought about professional intervention? Hey, do you remember when we wrote all that emotional stuff on Day 4? Maybe you should go back and read that today, just to recall why it is that you are trying to move forward in the first place.

And don't forget to keep taking notes about the stuff you want to speak to your ex about! Every question and every statement that comes to mind, write it down at the back then put it away like a trooper. These thoughts are for safekeeping and are very important, especially the part where we *DO NOT* pass this information to the ex just yet no matter how brilliant your most recent epiphany was. Let it stew on paper for a little longer. You're building a solid case, remember? Never take a shot until you have fully loaded a gun with all six rounds, yeah?

"Hearts can break. Yes, hearts can break. Sometimes I think it would be better if we died when they did, but we don't." — Stephen King, Hearts in Atlantis

The final bit of text for today is to remind you about that Emotional Ladder from Day 3. Locate the feeling which best describes your general emotional state, then jot it down. Choose from the following:

The Emotional Ladder

1. Liberation!
2. Hopefulness and Excitement
3. Relief and Satisfaction
4. Boredom
5. Lost Confusion
6. Irritation, Frustration, and Impatience
7. Sadness, Loneliness, and Longing
8. Doubtfulness and Discouragement
9. Furious Anger
10. Vengeful Hatred
11. Destructive Hatred
12. Jealousy
13. Fearful Anxiety
14. Unlovable Worthlessness
15. Utter Devastation and Depression

Got that? Done that? Look back at your notes from Day 3, what emotion did you write down back then? Have you improved at all? Have you stayed the same? Have you perhaps even dropped lower? Do not worry about the outcome so much, as the only aspect of any importance is that you are completely honest with yourself. And, seriously, do not stress if it feels like this isn't getting any better, because we're only at the end of the first week! We've still got a few tricks up our sleeves, believe you me you me.

But for now, do as we did before. After you've selected your current emotion, look at the point above, and that is your current goal. The emotional objective. Do whatever it takes to get there. Research the definition of that term, and calculate an imaginative way to climb to it, even if you have to get weird. If you achieve it with ease, then reach for the next one. If you struggle to get there, at least you gave it a go. And if you simply can't improve your situation, that's cool too. Tomorrow is a new day.

If nothing else, try to remember to catch your emotions in the act next time they are upsetting your vibe, then come back to this ladder to assist your gradual climb out. Because that's why it's here.

"Your emotions are the slaves to your thoughts, and you are the slave to your emotions." — Elizabeth Gilbert, Eat Pray Love

And so to recap...

Today was the first reevaluation day which will be unique to everybody. It's a time to pause and reflect, looking back over the journey and calculating which aspects require more attention before moving forward.

Flip through your notebook. Which days deserve a second go? What's the plan?

Day 10
The Rebounding Technique

Day 10
The Rebounding Technique

"Fishing is boring, unless you catch an actual fish, and then it is disgusting." — Dave Barry

We have just about reached phase two of our master plan. We've finished installing a decent security system within us and immediately around us, and now the time is upon us to start moving forward. Very. Slowly.

One of the most common versions of breakup advice (and I'm confident that you've already heard it from all sorts of mouths) is to get back on the horse. Another variation is when unimaginative people inform you of how many fish there are in the sea. The problem with these so-called "insightful" consultations is that they are far too preoccupied with animals when we need to be looking at humans here.

The rebound technique is essential to address, as one highly debated, trademark heartbreak manoeuvre. Many intelligent minds have weighed into the argument with intensely conflicting opinions, each pointing out the advantages/disadvantages of the hasty acceleration, neither answer universally accepted as right or wrong. Which is why I refuse to get involved, and would rather spend today picking apart the details surrounding this method and then leaving it in your perfectly capable hands to make the decision you feel is best for you.

"The best way to get over a man is to get under a new one." — Ryan Turner (played by Charlie Sheen), Good Advice

The above quote is a classic! It's funny! Yet at the same time, this is a genuine method of attack against breakup trauma. Many interviewees

I met wholeheartedly swore that this quick shag procedure is *"the only way"* to get over someone else, which is a bold declaration that comes with some merit. As you are probably well aware at this point, a romantic split is highly destructive to someone's self-worth. It's a place beneath the rubble where an individual may doubt their stock value, plagued by those terrible thoughts that no one will find them attractive again. On that train, the attention of someone else's body could provide the exact ego validation you require to get your head higher out of this swamp. Furthermore, those revenge seekers will find that nothing sends the spear of retribution into their ex's heart quite as swiftly as this little fling routine. As a result, if such an opportunity arises, by all mean, jump right into it. It's ok if that's what you want to do. And, honestly, what could go wrong?

"Rebound relationships are a great way to boost your ego while completely shattering an innocent person's life." — Unknown

Well, of course, there are a lot of things that could go wrong, and while my intention is not to complicate your life or sway your adult decision in any way, it is my duty to keep you updated on all corners of this world. So take the following information however you see fit.

The primary problem with the fleeting intercourse of affection works similarly to the drugs and alcohol we discussed earlier. It's like a single dose of Prozac, treating the symptoms as a temporary mechanism of relief. But when it's over, you're still alone, and it was probably lousy sex anyway. Even worse, you may latch onto this poor new individual who was simply looking for some fun, because you are a wounded animal who doesn't even know who they are, nothing but a gaping heart begging for care. After the act, you may feel used yet useless at the same time. It's a dangerous fire to be poking at right now.

Oh wait, there is something even worse than that! What if this person gets the wrong idea and they latch on to *you?* Then you've hurt someone because you weren't looking for anything serious, just a little bit of intimacy or perhaps a revenge lay, and now you've spread your pain onto some other innocent individual. Shame on you!

Oh, actually, there is something even worse! You *both* latch onto one another! And then you enter a relationship when you are in no position to give your love out because your shattered heart lies in pieces within your abdomen. You are basically handing them a pile of broken porcelain and saying *"here, fix this"* and maybe they'll glue it back together, but it'll probably be all wrong because they don't know what it used to look like. And your gut instinct won't fully trust them anyway because you've recently had all of your emotional investment in someone brutally severed, which will make you a terrible lover. You run the risk of repeating all of these same mistakes, and then I'll meet you back on Day 1.

> *"Until you get comfortable with being alone, you'll never know if you're choosing someone out of love or loneliness." — Mandy Hale*

All of which is a very pessimistic attitude on my part, and is not necessarily what will happen. Maybe you'll find your soulmate tomorrow. Maybe a quick visit to some stranger's bed will clear your head right up. These are your pathways to calculate. However, if you want my humble opinion, the best way to respect yourself and everyone else is to see this thing through. Ride this breakup out, feel the pain until it goes away. Rediscover yourself, and then you will be in a stronger position to pick a mate who is not only perfect for you but also joins your life when you are healthy enough to treat them fairly as a whole. Meeting someone new may be the quickest ice pack of relief to your burnt skin, but you are a broken toy, and bowing down to the first dribbling set of genitalia won't solve anything. Abstain, and read this book to the end first. It may not be the easiest approach, true, but it is the most admirable and dignified.

With that in mind, I am not known for turning down sex myself, so who am I to tell you what to do?

"I always say don't make plans, make options." — Jennifer Aniston

Alright, glad we got that chat out of the way. Now let's have some fun because, after all, you're single now! And being single does come with the exciting opportunities for exploring the idea of new people, so let's give that a go, just to see. But don't worry, we're going to approach any views on the dating game so slowly that it will be like walking on ice barefoot. Which is my poetic way of saying *watch your step, or you're gonna plummet to your death*. I mean, obviously not your literal death, but like, really negative vibes.

Often what we crave in these times, at its most rudimentary form, is just a bit of physical contact. There are many other healthier ways to obtain this, just so long as it's appropriate and consensual, you understand? Hug people who like to be hugged by you. Hug all of your friends hello, proper tight hugs, they will love it. If you are more into a handshake type of exchange, exaggerate it, by holding their hand in both of your hands as you do so, or by placing your other hand on their shoulder. Even in a work environment, make it your mission to shake everyone's hand for a whole day. If people think you're behaving weird, just be completely upfront, and tell them that today is the day when you shake everyone's hand or even give out free high-fives. They will probably find it quite amusing.

If all else fails, get a massage. That way, you are supporting someone's business and unwinding your stress all through the magic of human touch—win/win. Then there's the power of animals. If you pass a dog or have a pet, play with this creature for as long as you can. The animal will adore you for it and will give you all the attention you require until your heart fills up with love. I can't emphasise this point enough, as many people I interviewed for this book swore by the healing therapy of their fluffy friends. Seek this out. Who needs humans, anyway?

"Our perfect companions never have fewer than four feet."
— Colette

Except, of course, we do need humans, because we *are* humans, and it's quite tricky to have a two-sided intelligent conversation with a cat, trust me, I have tried. Which is why we are about to add some weight onto this momentum, prepare yourself.

But before we even discuss this, I must underline with all of my fibres that **the following text is for educational purposes only**. Read it, and if it doesn't seem like a comfortable downward flow for you right now, pass through it with your arms crossed. Do not ever do anything that you are not ready to do, because that would be like flicking at the matchsticks which are holding you up right now. You could fall, and you could set yourself on fire.

Regardless, looking forward is necessary, because looking forward is the best way to look, especially if you don't want to walk into things. You may already find the prospect of a new potential lover exciting, and this emotion itself is healthy. I encourage it! By optimistically focusing on a positive future, you are helping yourself to leave the dark past behind, and that is the whole idea. However, I must implore once again, that you are *definitely not* equipped to commit to another relationship right now. How could I know such a thing? Because you are reading this book.

That said, let's discuss ways you can still eagerly face towards an eventual promise of a new lover with minimal threat to your tender insides, using the following suggestions as a rope to pull yourself a little further out of the quicksand without bursting your stitches.

"People tend to look at dating sort of like a safari—like they're trying to land the trophy." — Henry Cloud

I know of one creepy little exercise you might like to try. Scroll through your entire list of friends (either via social media or a phone book or your memory or whatever is your preferred medium), and then make a note of those people who are relatively attractive to you. Perhaps these are people who you may have once had a chance with. Perhaps these are people who you would've hooked up with if you had been single at the time. Perhaps these are people you have already hooked up with briefly before, but it never went anywhere. Even if some potential candidates are better than others, this does not matter. What matters is that you come out of the other side with a list of five to ten people that you somewhat fancy. Naturally, it's in your best interest to avoid any of those individuals who are a mutual connection between you and your ex. That is still too close to the place we are trying to escape. But everyone else is fair game (within reason, use your best judgement).

And then here comes the scary bit. One by one, send these people a message. I mean, don't send them all today, that would be unreasonable. Rather, send one per day for the next ten or so days, if you feel up to it.

The intention of your message should not be about getting laid. The purpose of your letter should not even be about meeting up, for you will reek of desperation and any further rejection is the last thing you need right now. Do not open yourself to that possibility. Do not mention your recent breakup whatsoever. Instead, you should simply say something to the effects of *"Hey! You randomly popped into my head/I had a surreal dream about you last night/I noticed you went to Fiji recently and I was hoping for tourist tips. How are you?"*. Essentially just that. Nothing more, nothing less.

The responses you receive will vary. Some might be non-existent. Some might be boring, offering you one-worded answers and the conversation may end abruptly. Others could engage in fascinating chatter, and you should reciprocate. But no matter what the exchange, remember that this is about finding your footing again and opening yourself up to new discussions and good-looking friends. It is not about finding the next person to date. If a meet-up with a hot acquaintance comes of it, that's fine, add them to the list of weekly social participants discussed on Day 7, but keep in mind that this is not the primary objective. You are merely re-accessing the fun flirty side of your personality, reminding yourself of your worth. And what's more, you are doing so with people where there's already some sort of a rapport, minimising the awkwardness and desperation one may find on a dating website, for example.

"She is resisting the Internet idea...because she doesn't want to one day tell her children that she posted an ad on the Internet, interviewed twenty-five hopeful candidates, and finally their father turned up and looked good in comparison with the rest of them. It just doesn't seem right." — Jenny Colgan, Little Beach Street Bakery

While we're on that topic, I wouldn't rule out dating websites either (which includes all of those funky apps filled with carefully chosen picture angles as we swipe away based on superficial reasons). Once again, if you dip into this realm, do not do so to find a partner. That should be the last thing on your mind. This is just for fun. It's all about enjoying the process of setting up your profile and exaggerating your most desirable traits or being brutally honest about your faults, then noting the vast amount of characters available on the market. There are tons! Literally millions of contestants, a massive portion of whom are waiting for someone just like you. Silently stalk and judge these people based on trivial reasons without shame, because you're heartbroken, so you deserve some shallow behaviour right now. Message people if you like them, respond to people who message you. Be flirtatious. But do not take this course seriously, because your heart isn't ready for more love or denial just yet. Rather, poke around the world of singledom just to take a look.

Remember: whether a dating site or friends list, you are still walking on that ice. Do not rush this part of the process, or you may fall. The only reason I address this concept so early is to equip you with opinions to steer you in a direction better suited for you. But, in truthfulness, this piece of the journey should be left at arm's length for as long as possible. Harmless messaging is great for self-confidence, and casually toying with chemistry is part of human nature. But running out into the open with *"I'm single and ready"* pasted onto your forehead not only looks desperate, but will attract the wrong person, and the cycle may repeat itself. If you do happen to meet someone new who you think are worthy, play it cool and take it so slowly that it's almost frozen. Be honest with his person and tell them you're not there yet. Your priority is, at very least, to complete this book before jumping into anything else. Once this month is up (and if you feel strong enough for it), you can reflect on this day, and revisit the potential contender who expressed the most interest; who related to you on the deeper level; who spoke to you on a natural plain above the others. Only consider whether it's worth checking them out once you're healed. If someone is truly worthy of you, they'll understand the wait.

"Sex without love is a meaningless experience, but as far as meaningless experiences go, it's pretty damn good." — Woody Allen

And so to recap...

Today the time has come to evaluate your stance on rebounding. What are your thoughts on the matter? Are you curious about exploring this gift of newfound freedom? Or would you prefer to recover a little more first?

Once you have come to a solid conclusion, write down your choice and then detail any actions you will (or won't) be taking in this regard.

Day 11

Fix Up, Look Sharp

Day 11
Fix Up, Look Sharp

"If I want to knock a story off the front page, I just change my hairstyle." — Hillary Clinton

Did you ever think that getting over heartbreak would be this much fun?! Wait, what do you mean you aren't having fun? Well, don't worry about it. Because you'll be happy to know that we've just about covered the monotonous scope of all the necessary tasks, and we have reached the much more enjoyable parts of this book. No, really!

Starting with this: the first step towards becoming a brand new version of yourself is… to become a brand new version of yourself! And the easiest way to achieve this is to alter your outward appearance.

"When we are no longer able to change a situation, we are challenged to change ourselves." — Viktor E. Frankl

Now, I don't mean simply buying a new hat or something (although, by all means, buy a new hat or something). I mean literally redesigning every single aspect of your external presentation that you can think of, no matter how uncomfortable these ideas make you feel. The goal here is to be unrecognisable whilst completely revamping your swag until you look fresh and oh-so-amazing.

Alright, so take a deep breath, grab your diary, and under today's headline, start jotting down thoughts of how you could overhaul your current look.

Here are just some suggestions for varying budgets:

- Get your hair cut into a new style.
- Dye your hair a different colour that you've never had before.

- Start wearing glasses if you wear contacts or contacts if you wear glasses.
- Wear coloured contacts no matter your eyesight.
- Pluck your eyebrows into a neat, presentable state.
- Girls, watch some new makeup tutorials online to change your faceplant.
- Boys, have you ever considered guyliner? The emo-goth look? Don't knock it until you try it? *(I went down this route myself, embarrassing)*
- Grow or shave your beard in a new way, if you can do such things.
- Get a facial piercing or any piercing really.
- Get your teeth polished.
- Get a new flashy necklace or bracelet or wristwatch or ankle chain or ring.
- Buy new clothes, give the old ones to charity.
- Or put away your new clothes, go back to the old ones you haven't worn in a while, perhaps finding funky ways to modify them.
- Girls, paint your nails and toenails a new colour.
- Boys, paint your nails and toenails a new colour too, get freaky with it.
- Keep all nails trimmed, or potentially grow them, but always maintain a level of cleanliness.
- Consider a bold accessory, like a cape or a walking stick or a bow tie or a hair flower.
- Get that tattoo you were considering a year ago.
- Shave your pubic hair into an exciting shape.
- Get an extra limb sewn onto your body if you're into that, whatever.

"A woman who cuts her hair is about to change her life."
— Coco Chanel

If your fashion sense is notoriously atrocious and you do not have any confidence in your taste, then I recommend chatting to a trendy friend. Alternatively, compile a list of three to four celebrities who you admire. Research what they wore to a recent ceremony, and amalgamate those ideas to create a super new you.

If the result petrifies you and you would rather die than leave the house like that, then don't leave the house like that. Simply keep exploring new avenues, experimenting until you find fresh additions which work for you, pushing yourself outward from your comfort zone, piece by piece, without having an anxiety attack. Your friends may worry that you've lost the plot, but they (and you) will get used to these alterations soon enough. And that's not what we're doing here anyway. What we're doing here is taking the time and attention to create a new personal brand, and you will almost immediately notice how the world starts to change around you.

"You can never be overdressed or overeducated." — *Oscar Wilde*

I know I don't need to spell this out for you, but I will anyway: by dedicating yourself to this step, no matter how much of a mess your brain is in, you will appear reborn. You will look better, and you will feel better accordingly. Furthermore, as a nifty little side effect, your social media photos will improve (because you should change your profile images as soon as the new you is unveiled) and this will bless your lonely heart with more attention. Not to mention that (heaven forbid!) if you happen to have an accidental run-in with your ex, this gleaming demeanour will knock them back as the worms of jealousy eat their organs from the inside out (if you care about such things).

Start planning this right now (like, right now!) and ensure that you make at least one change to your appearance per day, gradually edging towards total reinvention. Trust me, this move is freakin' powerful, and this was the day which I loved the most during my journey.

"And now, I'm just trying to change the world, one sequin at a time."
— Lady Gaga

And so to recap...

Using the examples provided as inspiration, write out a list of changes you are willing to make to your appearance. Then pick one, and follow through with it today.
Make a plan to keep up these adjustments, one every day until you are satisfied that you look completely refreshed and reborn.

Day 12
There's No Place Like Home

Day 12
There's No Place Like Home

"I live in my own little world. But it's ok, they know me here." — Lauren Myracle

Thanks to our friendly conversation yesterday, you should have already set some cogs in motion which will overhaul your outward appearance. With that momentum churning, we are going to slowly push this idea further outwards, starting with your house.

On a quick side note, I do have to address those of you who are still currently living with your ex. I urge you to read this chapter as anyone would, and apply it to any space you can. I will assume that you're making plans where one of you is moving out, because if you are not, then you have more significant concerns on your hands. To put it bluntly, you will never escape this heartbreak rut with this person's presence perpetually reminding you of your failed relationship. I repeat: you cannot live with your ex; otherwise, none of this book will work. I know it's always more complicated than I could put on paper, but if you can get them out, then get them out, and the power of this chapter will be immeasurable in comparison. However, if you cannot get them out, then you need to move somewhere else, and in doing so, you will have already completed all of your work for this chapter. You will be in the ideal position of a clear domestic slate, and even though it may not feel like it, you'd be luckier than most.

On that topic, let's take this one step further into the realms of insanity, and by all means, feel free to leave regardless of your home situation! Move house! Runaway! Go on a faraway trip! Change country! Leave it all behind! If I had the courage and finances to do that in my time of peril, I totally would have (and I since have). What else is life about? Even just a quick holiday to a new environment will be like viewing a masterpiece painting after staring at a brick wall for the longest of times.

"Everyone thinks of changing the world, but no one thinks of changing himself." — Leo Tolstoy

For the rest of us who cannot afford this luxury and are currently living in a separate space to that of an ex, then today's journey is built just for you. In one sentence, this is the plan: your entire house needs to change. Everything that isn't nailed to the floor needs to move position. Everything that can be replaced needs to be thrown away. Everything that can be needs to be attacked with paint. Everything. Changed. Get the vibe? If not, below is a list of ideas to inspire you.

- Pick a colour or a few matching colours that you love, and focus on placing that specific shade in your line of vision as much as possible.
- Change the wall colour of every room you have permission to paint.
- Move your bed into another position, perhaps even to force you to start sleeping on the other side of it.
- Buy loads and loads of pillows, and put them everywhere.
- Change your bedspread to an opposite pattern or colour.
- Install canopy drapes around your bed.
- Move all tables, desks, and cupboards into different positions, just to see.
- Swap your sock drawer and your underwear draw around, you rebel, you.
- Buy a new floor mat.
- Hang beads in your doorway like an old school hippie.
- Move your posters/paintings around or replace them or even turn them upside down.
- Replace all small ornaments.
- Get a fishbowl.
- Ask an artist friend to paint an optimistic mural on your

bedroom wall.

- Put any clutter in boxes, and get them out of sight.
- Stick up fairy lights everywhere.
- Get one of those LED toilet lights.
- Place a weird covering over one of your lights somewhere to change the hue of the room.
- Purchase a lamp to summon light from another angle.
- New curtains.
- Relocate your bedroom to another room if you have that option.
- Move all electronics out of your room and set them up in another.
- Change the background wallpaper of your computer and smartphone, along with any ringtones and alert noises.
- Candles!
- Incense!
- Plants!
- Oils!
- Scented anything!

"I can't change the direction of the wind, but I can adjust my sails to always reach my destination." — Jimmy Dean

This task will not happen overnight, but for today, look at the above examples and start writing down which ones are practical to your circumstances. Create a rough to-do list of possibilities, adding to it whenever inspiration strikes, then religiously tick off one item every single day, slowly moving towards the ultimate goal. And what's the ultimate goal? It's to wake up one morning and experience that fleeting confusion that you aren't quite sure where you are. That's when you know you've done it. You've escaped a rut without ever leaving. But you better get working right now, because the more gradual this change, the less of a chance you have of surprising yourself.

The benefits of this exercise are the same as yesterday. You are creating a brand new place for the brand new you to come home to; a fresh resting habitat which will lead to a fresh mindset. Furthermore, this specific venture does come with the bonus of exorcising any haunting memories of past lovers, dusting their presence from the corners, obscuring any stubborn recollections associated with any particular area. Hence why I must emphasise that you pay careful attention to any regions of your house designated for their stuff. If they had a drawer for their clothes, or if they had a spot they'd always dump their bags when they visited, or if they had a shelf where they kept their toothbrush and face cream, you need to put something in that place which you love to look at, pulling your brain in a different direction. This small action will gradually erode any agonising power that little place once yielded, now replacing it with a friendly item of your choosing. Simples!

"Once you replace negative thoughts with positive ones, you'll start having positive results." — Willie Nelson

If you don't mind, to end with, I would like to share a beautiful personal experience I had when executing this step. Following the procedure, I was moving my exceptionally heavy bookshelf from one side of my room to the other, and then all hell broke loose. I lost my balance, and the shelf tipped over. Books and DVDs and the like rained painfully upon my head as I screamed, trying the best I could to not be crushed and killed beneath my own furniture. Do you think my ex was on my mind when this was going down? No. I was much more concerned with not dying.

"The difficulty lies not so much in developing new ideas as in escaping from old ones." — John Maynard Keynes

And so to recap...

Much like the change to your appearance, the same effect can be enjoyed at home too! Read over the examples and then evaluate your house, making a list of every aspect which you can alter. And then start altering! One point, every day, until you can't remember where you are.

Day 13
Clean Your Insides By Cleaning Your Outsides

Day 13
Clean Your Insides By Cleaning Your Outsides

"If you want to change the world, start off by making your bed. If you make your bed every morning, you will have accomplished the first task of the day. It will give you a small sense of pride, and will encourage you to do another task, and another, and another. By the end of the day, that one task completed will have turned into many tasks completed. Making your bed will also reinforce the fact that the little things in life matter. If you can't do the little things right, you'll never be able to do the big things right. If, by chance, you have a miserable day, you will come home to a bed that is made. That you made. And a made bed gives you encouragement that tomorrow will be better." —William H. McRaven

While you march along with your daily steps, pruning your feathers and turning your room inside out, I have another little task to throw in the mix. It may be a little less exciting than the previous two, but it's still worthy of the conversation.

For at least 15 minutes a day, you should focus upon the organisation and cleaning of an area in your house. If you tell me that you don't have 15 minutes, then I will politely suggest that you are telling fibs. Make 15 minutes appear out of thin air, even if it comes from your sleep or dinner or TV time. It isn't too much to ask. However, I'll play along, and if it is genuinely too much to ask, bring it down to 10 minutes. Or even five. Once you begin to grasp the power of this suggestion, you'll probably find yourself upping it to 15 on your own accord anyway. You'll see.

"Who has time? Who has time? But then if we do not ever take time, how can we ever have time?" — The Merovingian; The Matrix Reloaded

Make a list of chores you've been meaning to get around to but have procrastinated. Areas that are begging for a cleaning. Objects which need fixing. Papers which need to systemisation. Take a walk around your house and look for annoyances. Add to this list whenever a new idea comes to you. And if you get stuck, steal from the following list of suggestions:

- Pick the hair out from your hairbrush.
- Go through your clothing and give any items to charity that you haven't worn for a year.
- Finally match up your pairs of socks.
- Clean your shoes.
- Do your laundry.
- Organise the folders on your computer.
- Reformat your hard drive.
- Organise your bank statements.
- Clear out your backpack or purse.
- Replace batteries and light bulbs wherever needed.
- Glue any loose scraps of precious paper into an actual scrapbook.
- Alphabetise your book or vinyl collection.
- Take that dead clock to the clock shop man.
- Mow your lawn.
- Clear out your garage.
- Clear out your fridge.
- Scrub out your oven.
- Wipe all countertops and cupboards.
- Clean the toilet.
- Scrub that mould between your tiles.
- Remove the hair from the drainpipe.

- Clean all household mirrors.
- Throw away those empty bottles in the shower.
- Sort through the products in the cupboard under your sink.
- Distribute the mail if you're in a shared household, or if you have some of the neighbour's mail kicking about, deliver it.
- Vacuum.
- Dust.
- Mop.

"You do not get gold stars for cleaning your toilet. In actual life, there is a depressing lack of stickers." — Alexandra Petri Read

Look, I don't care if you're the cleanest of all neat freaks on this planet Earth, there is always something to do each day. Get creative with it. Go deeper. Start applying this to your space at work. Clean up other people's mess, they will appreciate it, or even better, it may embarrass them into being more considerate next time. The possibilities are endless.

Once you've decided on your daily cleaning task for today (yes, today), set a timer for 14 minutes and then tackle this chore head-on, do not hesitate. As soon as the 14 minutes have run out, you have one minute to finish up, and that's it. If you have to leave a job half-finished, that's not a problem, pick it up again tomorrow. I've taken a week to clean a shower before, and that's fine. Although that said, you may be surprised at how often you'll want to continue without breaking the flow, and in those cases, keep on going!

"I love cleaning, weird but true. It really relaxes me." — Jessie J

You should also decide on one day a week (Wednesday?) where you spend your 15 minutes rushing over all the areas you've already sorted. Regular revisiting will maintain the order and won't let your hard work slip; otherwise, it's kinda pointless.

And now I wonder: are you currently sitting there, reading this chapter in fury, wondering why the hell I am asking you to clean up when you're clearly in pain? Is this the last thing in the world you feel like doing right now? Who do I think I am, your mom? No, let me assure you that I am not your mom. Furthermore, I will explain not one but two solid reasons why this daily practice will work wonders towards your heart healing, so get ready to be blown away.

"I look forward to spring cleaning and putting things in their place. It's therapeutic for me." — Kimora Lee Simmons

The first reason is that cleaning is a therapeutic distraction with a constructive outcome. It often feels as if a messy environment reflects your messy mind, and by confronting it bit by bit, the end result is so tangible that you can literally measure it, punctuated by the full stop of accomplishment. At the end of each chore, you can stand back with pride that you've made a difference for the better, keeping yourself useful, giving your day purpose, and tasting the satisfaction of your hands well spent. You will feel lifted by it, guaranteed.

The second reason is that gradually, your place of rest will fall into better and better shape, creating a much happier habitat for you when you come home. Seriously, 15 minutes a day minimum is all you need, they will add up faster than you can you comprehend, and you will adore the benefits. Your house will smell better. There will be less chance of getting sick as you murder any lurking bacteria. And your friends will love coming over because everything looks so sparkly all the time. Win-Win-Win-Win-Win.

"Cleanliness is next to Godliness" — Ancient Hebrew Proverb

And so to recap...

Just like the two days previous, the idea here is to analyse your current situation and write a list of changes you wish to tackle. Use the provided examples and walk around your house until you have a decent collection of chores to perform.

Once you have this, decide on the best time of day to spend 15 minutes on these tasks, and commit yourself to the process of developing a better home! After a few short days, you'll understand why!

Day 14
Routine Routine Routine

Day 14
Routine Routine Routine

"We are what we repeatedly do. Excellence then, is not an act, but a habit." — Aristotle

Perhaps you've realised this, but a large part of what we're doing here is trying to beat your brain at its own game. We achieve this by using one of the most effective means we've got: confusion! When we start to look different, and our house starts to look different, then the wires of your mind are going to start thinking that you *are* different. And once you've convinced your mind that you are different then congratulations, you're different. In that regard, we have one final card to play, and that is to mess around with your daily routine. That should show your brain who's boss around here!

The following advice may sound contradictory at first, but what we are hoping to do is to build the tightest routine you can tolerate, whilst destroying it at the same time. If you are wondering how to do that, do not worry, for I am going to tell you, otherwise there would be no point to what I just said. Let's start by looking at building the routine first before we tear it down.

"The secret of your future is hidden in your daily routine." — Mike Murdock

A daily routine is a beneficial structure to have in your life irrespective of breakups. If you feel like having a routine was never your strongest point or not something you are even interested in, that's fine, but I am still going to try to sell it to you. Be open!

The power behind a routine is that it keeps your brain marching forward in a militant fashion, getting stuff done and maximising the value of your time, wasting nothing. In turn, this perpetual motion does not often allow your mind the luxury of pausing and taking stock of your life. This strategy is ideal during a heartbreak period, because whenever you let your thoughts wander off on their own, they will run straight back to your ex, and you will feel depressed again. Instead, let's keep the wheels spinning, as this will be more difficult for depression to catch up with.

The best (or only) way to achieve this, is to use a work diary or a calendar or one of the many organisational apps available for today's modern world (Googling *"organisational phone apps"* should provide the latest options best tailored for you). We do this because we want to get your schedule out of your head. Once you've done so, you won't have to remember anything anymore. Let the paper/machine remember your life for you! Less clutter bouncing around your skull! Not to mention, there is something strangely satisfying about ticking things off a to-do list one-by-one. Armed with this tool, plan the forthcoming day on an hour to hour basis. Plan for every moment of your time until your whole 24 hours has no space to breathe. Unless, of course, you want some space to breathe. Then schedule that in somewhere too.

I understand that this may sound like it will destroy all the spontaneity out of your free spirit, but be logical about that thought. If you suddenly have the urge to jump on a plane and fly to Alaska, then tear your daily list up and do that. Nobody is stopping you; I wouldn't dare. But if you know that you're not going to Alaska tomorrow then you run the risk of being a little bit lost, a little bit aimless, and as a result, likely to stumble into a dark place of emotions and memories. Why not give this a try instead? Plan your days, always have something to do, no time to waste. Worst case scenario, you can't face it, you collapse, you feel depressed, you try again. Best case scenario, your day rushes passed and you get so much done that you have a bunch of concrete achievements to show for your waking hours. And what's more, you were far too busy to even think about whoever that was back then. Exhausting? Damn right. You'll sleep better that way.

"I'm not ignoring you. I'm busy building my empire." — Moosa Rahat

Here are some specific tasks that should become a part of your routine, performed at the same time every day:

- Waking up, same time, every day.
- Have a designated half hour to respond to personal emails, same time, every day.
- Eat lunch, same time, every day.
- Read this book, same time, every day.
- Work on your appearance, same time, every day, as we discussed before.
- Work on changing your room around, same time, every day, as we discussed before.
- Work on cleaning bits of your house for 15 minutes, same time, every day, as we discussed before.
- Eat dinner, same time, every evening.
- Go to bed, same time, every night.

Bonus content: To super-slide your timeline along, practice the art of simple multitasking. Here are some tips you can apply right now:

- Answer your emails on the toilet or while waiting for the bus.
- Brush your teeth in the shower.
- Check your social media while you eat breakfast or commute.
- Read or write or plan your day on public transport.
- If you drive to work, record voice notes of reminders or ideas.
- Turn on the kettle before you go pee.
- Preheat the oven while you open your mail or clear your inbox.
- Eating dinner can double up as a social occasion, or the perfect time to watch your favourite TV show this evening.

Once you get the hang of this system, your time will turn into a playground as you realise how powerful the results can be with a minimal amount of effort. As we've covered before, even just 15 minutes a day dedicated to something will add up insanely fast, and before you know it, you'll get something big done. Just think about it. Fifteen minutes, five days a week works out to be 65 hours a year. That's like working on something for almost three days straight, without doing anything else at all. Robert Louis Stevenson wrote the first draft of the *Strange Case of Dr Jekyll and Mr Hyde* in that time and it changed his life. Have fun with it, or don't bother.

"I travel a lot; I hate having my life disrupted by routine."
— Caskie Stinnett

Ok, so what about those of us who already abide by a strict routine? Was all of this a complete waste of reading? Well, I don't believe so, because truth be told, even the laziest of us have some version of a routine, it's human nature. And so while we're busy working out how to maximise this time, let's also take a look at the things we are already doing out of habit, and then mix those up just for laughs. Execute these ideas immediately to shake your tree:

- Change the sound of your alarm.
- Change your brand of toothpaste.
- Brush your teeth with your other hand tonight.
- Do your hair before you put your shoes on, or vice versa.
- Walk a different way to the train station to drive a new route to work.
- Eat a lunch you've never had before.
- Eat your lunch somewhere you've never eaten before.
- Change your usual variation of the *"good morning"* phrase to something completely different, such as *"hey there"* or *"yo!"*
- Swap your gym days around.
- If you usually call your mom on a Tuesday, throw her off and call her on Monday, it'll blow her mind.
- Start regularly using a different bathroom at work.

- Do your grocery shopping in a store you've never been in before.
- Peel a banana differently.
- Turn right instead of left.
- Look up instead of down.

"A change is as good as a rest" — Proverb

These are just silly general ideas which could loosely apply to most people, which is why you're going to have to be observant about your behaviour over the next couple of days to squeeze the best juice out of this task. Locate the most potent habitual acts which define your brand of routine, then change them. And no matter how pointless all of this may seem, there is legitimate science behind it. The disruption of repeated processes strengthens the memory, builds willpower, activates creativity, and (most importantly, for us) scrambles your reality until you forget to think whatsoever.

To conclude: when you combine the last four days, keeping all of their motors running throughout your hours and taking notes every time an idea hits, these singular units will conspire together, forming a massive force, one which could even have enough power to surge you the furthermost distance away from your slump. Perhaps even more than anything else in this book. Your entire life is becoming refurbished, polished shiny with that brand new car smell, racing forward in a different direction. This exciting prospect is not only morphing you into a more modern version of yourself who achieves so much during their day but is also the perfect method to eradicate all reminders of you-know-who (sorry to remind you of them right there though). Dedicate yourself to this process, and the rewards will come fast and strong.

"I understand there's a guy inside me who wants to lay in bed, smoke weed all day, and watch cartoons and old movies. My whole life is a series of stratagems to avoid, and outwit, that guy."
— Anthony Bourdain

And so to recap...

Today was about locating that unique balance between building a routine which propels your days along, while also changing every small detail of your daily habits that you can.
Start by planning the next few days on an hourly basis, while also keeping a keen eye on any regular behaviours which you can easily alter, taking note of what excites you the most.

Day 15
Look Out For Number One

Day 15
Look Out For Number One

"Just think of all those women on the Titanic who said, 'No thank you' to dessert that night. And for what?!" — Erma Bombeck

Oh my gosh, can you believe we're already halfway through this book? It's true! Just look at the number! 15 is half of 30.

Let's celebrate! Let's take it easy! You deserve it. You've done so well. Which is why, today, we're going to explore the relief of pampering oneself and indulging in the things you most fancy. Don't ever say that I don't do anything for you.

"Pampered vanity is a better thing perhaps than starved pride."
— Joanna Baillie

Today is the day where all the other days temporarily don't matter. Today is the day where you take a break and put aside this tiresome process of trying to fix yourself all of the time. Let it go. Spoil yourself! Be spontaneous. Be impulsive. Do so guilt-free.

Start by making a list of things you love. Simple things. Things you could easily organise and execute, if not today, then by making a plan to do so very soon. I mean, I understand that I just sprung this upon you, and you can't shut off your whole life just because I said so, but you can at least begin the fun by grabbing your notebook and writing out a quick checklist. Scribble down a few luxuries you would like to pursue, then slowly tick them off throughout this journey. Here are some suggestions to get you moving:

- Call in sick to work.
- Get a massage or a manicure.
- Go to the nearest park and read a book.

- Go to the nearest ice cream parlour or eat a huge slice of cake.
- Binge-watch your favourite TV show whilst wrapped in blankets and ordering takeaway.
- Drink more tea than you ever have in your life.
- Take a nap.
- Go to the theatre or cinema.
- Go to the mall and explore a bit of retail therapy or do some serious online shopping.
- Call your most reckless friend and tell them it's on.
- Get on a train to a place you've never seen.
- Find an amusement park and ride the scariest roller coaster.
- Take a looooong bubble bath.
- Swim in the ocean.
- Seek out a dog or a cat to play with.
- Watch the sunset from the highest spot in your neighbourhood.

Obviously, trying to cover everything in one go would be the opposite of a relaxing time. So, after you write your list, pick one or two points you could easily achieve in the next few days, then plan out the rest of them, setting loose deadlines for when you need to complete them.

But wait, there's more! Now that you have this record of cool things you want to get done, there is a second (perhaps even superior) use for the list. As follows: if you ever feel yourself having an unfortunate flash of pain or a particularly miserable hour, flick back in your diary to this very day and randomly select a point you wrote down. Then do it. Such a quick inspired reaction of gratification could provide the much-needed relief to fix you right up, instantaneously.

"America is the first culture in jeopardy of amusing itself to death."
— John Piper, Don't Waste Your Life

Unfortunately, reality does exist too, sorry to be a downer. You don't want to go crazy and run off into the sunset then fall over into the deep end. There needs to be some limits set here. Bathing in chocolate or buying everything that catches your eye is nice, but if you pursue that every day then you will end up fat and broke. You won't feel too loving towards yourself at that point at all.

Instead, utilise this method with some reserved caution. By all means, push it as hard as you can today because today is your day! But after this point, only indulge in moderation. When you feel at your most hopeless, take a stand against the pain by turning it around and spoiling yourself, sending your insides the message that you love them after all. And when your spirits lift, stop this nonsense and continue with your recovery.

"Look out for Number One. If you don't, no one else will."
— Arnold Rothstein

And so to recap...

Give yourself some love! Shower your soul with affection! Take the day off and pamper! Make a list of things you'd rather be doing right now, then make a plan to do them right now!
And remember, whenever you're feeling low, you can always revisit this step for a quick sigh of relief.

Day 16
Reevaluation Day

Day 16
Reevaluation Day

"Reflect upon your present blessings, of which every man has many, not on your past misfortunes, of which all men have some." — Charles Dickens, A Christmas Carol and Other Christmas Writings

Another week has passed since we last reflected upon the journey behind us, so let's do that again. Where has our trip led us? Where should we be? Are there any of the previous steps where you don't feel like you reached your maximum capability? Today is the day to readdress those, looking back to specific intentions then attacking them from a fresh angle before we move forwards once again.

"Man cannot remake himself without suffering, for he is both the marble and the sculptor." — Dr. Alexis Carrel

From the beginning: how's the distance between you and your ex? Have you managed to evaporate all contact completely, or at least cut it down to the essential matters only? Speaking from experience and research, this can often be the most torturously tricky fight of the process, and so if you have messed up in weaker moments, take a deep breath, and clear the slate, beginning again. Go back to Day 5, reread it, put further barriers in place. It takes time, and you are not superhuman. On the other hand, if you have managed to keep this up, then good work!

Regardless, please don't forget to keep adding to the list of things you want to say to your ex *without* actually saying anything, as discussed on Day 4.

At this stage of the game, you should have met up with (or made

100% secure plans to meet up with) at least two friends on a one-on-one basis, using these social occasions to vent a little bit of pain without being too much of a bore. Are you behind on this? Message someone right now and schedule something in for the next few days!

Have you refrained from publicly broadcasting your sadness on social media? Have you been drinking too much? Have you been in touch with a professional? The degrees of your participation is dependent on your situation, but as long as you are making a determined effort and are seriously contemplating these proposals, then you are making progress. Just remember that you can lie to me, but you gotta be honest with yourself.

Let's look at the previous week. There should be a few tasks that you have implemented into your daily existence, and the immediate visual space around your person should have started to change rather dramatically. Have you made alterations to your personal appearance? Have people commented on elements of it? Is your bedroom starting to look like a different environment? Is it cleaner and more organised than it was seven days ago? Is your house more inviting than ever? Are you aware of your routine, and are you making changes to skew these habits off in different directions?

These processes will take time (mainly because you've only just started some of them), and certain ideas will come more natural than others. Take today to pause and note where you are with each of these tasks. Compliment yourself on the above factors which you feel you've made progress with while aiming your attention towards those you are less confident about, going back to reread their days if needs be, and trying to come up with a few new approaches of action. Remember that these steps are not here to make your life difficult! They are weaponry to nurture your current place of turmoil into one of complete rebirth, washing the bloodstains from the sheets of your heart, everything brand new for you to enjoy (and for the rest of the world to marvel at). Your recovery will surge forward with a fresh set of batteries.

"I don't know where I'm going, but I'm on my way." — Carl Sandburg

Only you know how you're doing, but if you've followed my suggestions religiously (and you really should be, don't forget why you are here), then your day-to-day life should already look a touch brighter no matter how dark your insides are. With that in mind, you'll be happy to know that from tomorrow, we start to attack your dirty soul with various cleansing products, so get ready for that.

But before we get to those exciting things, let us first look at that Emotional Ladder again. You know how it works. Locate the emotion on the following list which you've been hovering around the most lately, then focus on the vibe directly above, finding a way to climb up to it right now.

The Emotional Ladder

1. Liberation!
2. Hopefulness and Excitement
3. Relief and Satisfaction
4. Boredom
5. Lost Confusion
6. Irritation, Frustration, and Impatience
7. Sadness, Loneliness, and Longing
8. Doubtfulness and Discouragement
9. Furious Anger
10. Vengeful Hatred
11. Destructive Hatred
12. Jealousy
13. Fearful Anxiety
14. Unlovable Worthlessness
15. Utter Devastation and Depression

"Those who do not move, do not notice their chains."
— Rosa Luxemburg

How easy was it to achieve that today? Has your general state improved since the last time we did this exercise? Don't worry if it's all a big mess still, just be honest with yourself. Write down your answers and try to remember that this list exists. Any time you are having a terrible day, come back to it, look it over, analyse your insides and consider stepping upwards towards the next available zone. Or don't, it's up to you.

Get a good night's sleep. You're going to need it.

"I am a slow walker, but I never walk back." — Abraham Lincoln

And so to recap...

Today was another reevaluation day, granting you a moment to breathe and look over the pathway you have covered thus far. If there are any parts you feel like you could have done better with, now is the time to take a note and make a plan!

Day 17
Run Away From Your Demons

Day 17
Run Away From Your Demons

"If you don't take care of your body, where are you going to live?"
— Unknown

You knew this was coming! You just knew it! I'm sorry to be so predictable, I left it as late as I possibly could to build a trusted bond between us, but the time has come. We must face the well-documented facts that physical activity and raising your heartbeat is one of the fastest ways to pump the ache out from the same place.

No matter how this makes you feel, the good news is that it doesn't have to be that big of a deal, and it's up to you how much of this you want to adopt into your recovery. If the concept of exercise is a foreign conversation and the crippling agony of your breakup renders this as literally the last thing in the world you feel like doing, do not fear! As we can proceed so lightly that you will hardly even notice that it's happening.

"To keep the body in good health is a duty ... otherwise, we shall not be able to keep our mind strong and clear." — Buddha

How about doing a few reps of stomach crunches while your computer boots up? How about refusing to use elevators and always picking the stairs? Sometimes stairs move for us, we call these "escalators", but you should still walk up these too because then you'll get to where you're going much faster. Sweep your house enthusiastically. Pace around when talking on the phone. Explode into jumping jacks during the advert breaks. Dance to your favourite song. If you work at a computer, swap your desk chair for an exercise ball and set an hourly alarm to remind you to take a five-minute walk. Even going for a nature stroll or a brisk 10 minutes jog a day or a slow bike ride to the shop will help fill your lungs with that tasty natural oxygen and improve your mood drastically. Stretch. Take doggo for walkies. Consider your options when it comes to transport, perhaps a cycle would reduce your journey time (lack of traffic, shortcuts, etc.)? And when you get home, instead of slouching on the couch and playing video games, why not connect up an exergaming console instead and wiggle around the living room, shaking those calories right off your body. You will still experience that rewarding sense of success as you reach new levels and unlock bonus content, except in these games, the achievement is genuinely real.

"Exercise is really important to me—it's therapeutic. So if I'm ever feeling tense or stressed or like I'm about to have a meltdown, I'll put on my iPod and head to the gym or out on a bike ride along Lake Michigan with the girls." — Michelle Obama

There is this dangerous myth that exercise has to be boring, but that could not be further from the truth. If you can't fathom the mundane idea of running in circles, rather participate in a new after-work class every week until you find an activity which you consider to be the most enjoyable. The majority of places offer a "first class free" deal too, so exploit that.

Whether it be salsa dancing, ice skating lessons, basketball, modern dancing, swimming, hiking, boxing, mountain climbing… you name it, there is a place for you to do it. Plus there is an additional social benefit to this approach which will bring brand new faces with healthy outlooks into your circle. Use your notebook and give this some serious thought, please. You will feel lifted in record time.

For others, the infinite joy of fitness is not some brand new notion, and if this is the case, now it's time to up your game. Increase your routine, add another hour to your gym schedule, stack up those weights, beat your personal bests, really push yourself without causing injury. Expel all of that negative energy until you're too exhausted to feel anything at all. You know how it goes, so go.

"All truly great thoughts are conceived while walking."
— Friedrich Nietzsche, Twilight of the Idols

The benefits of exercise are so endlessly popular that you've heard them all before. We are animals designed to run for our lives, and so it's no surprise that our chemicals thrive on this behaviour. Long-term cardio exercise is proven to increase serotonin production, naturally alleviating depression as if magic. Furthermore, the norepinephrine in the brain increases, helping to battle against stress. You will also tire out, meaning an effortless fall into a much deeper slumber at night. And finally, your body will start to show results, which is kind of like Day 11 when we changed our decorative appearance for self-confidence, except this is at the root level. Look better naked! It's valuable for everyone.

Here's what you do. Starting today, make a list of any of physical activity that doesn't sound like a nightmare to you, whether it be a daily jog or a yoga class or 20 push-ups a day. Then start researching what's available in your area while studying your schedule, and make a solid plan of how you're going to start integrating them into your routine immediately. It would be best to dedicate *at least* 2.5 hours a week to some form of exercise, which includes *at least* one outside activity (no matter how short) per every day to air your cluttered head out. Your main goal here is to compete with yourself, pushing to improve upon your last score and progressively turning up the heat until your body aches rather than your heart.

Imagine your body at its peak condition. Imagine what certain people would think if they saw you like that. Hold on to that thought and then chase it.

"If you are in a bad mood, go for a walk. If you are still in a bad mood, go for another walk." — Hippocrates

I know some of you are reading this and are ready to skip ahead while ignoring everything I've just said, and I can't stop you. But what I will say is this: if you're spending your days on the couch watching TV whilst eating potato crisps and downing diet cola, you can't reasonably wonder why you're so depressed right now. Your brain and body are crying out for love and attention. Give it to them. Get them onto your side, and let nature do what it does. Simply put, exercise will make you happier or your money back.

"My grandmother started walking five miles a day when she was sixty. She's ninety-seven now, and we don't know where the heck she is."
— Ellen DeGeneres

And so to recap...

Today we discussed one of the most common suggestions to fight against heartbreak. These are common for a reason, so contemplate all of the options above, write down a simple exercise program that doesn't scare you, and start moving!

Day 18
A Piece Of Cake, Figuratively

Day 18
A Piece Of Cake, Figuratively

"The food you eat can be either the safest and most powerful form of medicine or the slowest form of poison." — Ann Wigmore

Following on predictably from yesterday's conversation, let's have a chit-chat about the food you're currently eating. I know this may seem boring, but the reason why it's boring is that you've heard it all before. And the reason why you've heard it all before is that there is truth to it.

Firstly, let's address comfort foods. Honestly, it's not all bad. Chocolate (the darker, the better) is loaded with chemicals such as tryptophan, phenylethylamine, and theobromine. These work together to make serotonin happiness, euphoric antidepressants, and a little bit of a motivating buzz. And at the end of the day, inhaling an entire pizza or an ice cream cake by yourself is still a delicious form of stimulation. Plus, if they help suffocate some heart pangs, then why not explore that defence once in a while?

The problem comes where this isn't exactly the healthiest of methods. You may rot your teeth, and you may become obese, which I am going to assume is not what you want? Furthermore, any immediate high you gain from stuffing your mouth full of processed goods (or bads, rather) will undoubtedly nose dive then crash when the sugar wears off and the guilt of what you've done sinks you down down down.

"Today, more than 95% of all chronic disease is caused by food choice, toxic food ingredients, nutritional deficiencies and lack of physical exercise." — Mike Adams

If it's any consolation, you can't blame yourself for these cravings. As per everything, the chemicals in your brain are malfunctioning at the moment, and they have recently experienced a drastic meltdown, liquified into a mess of cortisol, better known as the "stress hormone". It is this evil bugger who is begging you to bury its pain beneath salt and sugar and fats, and because it lives inside of your brain, you get confused, and you think it's your own thoughts. It's not! It's cortisol hacking you!

On the flip side, there will be some of us who find ourselves dealing with the opposite problem. Your appetite has packed its suitcase and left you; the very idea of eating anything makes you feel physically sick. You may think this is a great way to lose weight, and I applaud your positive outlook on life. However, this is even worse than comfort eating because it will damage your body as well as your happy neurochemicals much faster. Thankfully, this effect usually only lasts a few days after a breakup, and most people start eating again soon enough. Which is why, as we sit here on day 18, I must warn you: if you still haven't come right and have been eating much less than your recommended intake this whole time, then for the love of everything holy, you must speak to someone about this problem. Preferably a professional too. You may be in serious trouble which extends far beyond any pesky ex-partner pain. You need to fix this issue as your priority immediately.

"You are what you eat, so don't be fast, cheap, easy, or fake."
— Unknown

Ok, so now that we've got those unpleasantries out of the way, let's slowly sink back into reality. We live in a wonderful world where happiness is all around us. There are plenty of ways to eat a healthy, balanced, yummy diet which will promote chemical growth in your brain, turning you into a more cheerful person. It won't be like the instant explosion of adrenaline happiness from a big bag of cookies, but it also won't come with the nasty plummet at the end either. And each day that you eat better, you will feel better, and you will look better.

Start by *never* skipping breakfast (or any meal), as this will kick your daily metabolism into action from the starting line. Limit your junk snacking. And eat your dinner as early as possible to give your body a running chance to burn off those calories before you go to bed.

When it comes to what to eat, there are many studies which link foods to depression. These are either as a cause due to deficiency or an ally in fighting it. Here is a list of the best examples money can buy:

Fibre

What it does: Keeps the digestive system up and running correctly, helping you to face the day and avoiding any sluggishness.

Where to find it: Oatmeal. Whole wheat products. Beans.

Magnesium

What it does: Proven without a doubt to combat depression.

Where to find it: Nuts (almonds, cashews, peanuts, or Brazilian). Avocado. Black beans. Tofu.

Gastrointestinal Flora

What it does: Improves what's called the gut-brain axis, a scientifically proven mood-booster connection.

Where to find it: Yogurts (especially Greek). Certain fermented cheeses. Sauerkraut. Kombucha. Kimchi.

Tryptophan

What it does: An essential amino acid which the body uses to develop your happy neurotransmitter called serotonin.

Where to find it: Pumpkin seeds! Bananas. Eggs.

Lycopene

What it does: An anti-inflammatory substance proved to alleviate depression in many, many case studies.

Where to find it: Tomatoes! Tomato anything! Guavas. Watermelon.

General Antioxidants

What it does: Helps to lower stress.

Where to find it: Honey. Green tea. Pecan nuts. Berries (such as blueberries or strawberries).

Vitamin D

What it does: This is the sunshine vitamin! It fights off seasonal affective disorder (SAD, geddit?).

Where to find it: Mushrooms. Egg yolk. Cheese.

Vitamin C

What it does: A deficiency of this vitamin has been linked to symptoms suspiciously similar to that of depression.

Where to find it: Kale. Oranges. Red hot chili peppers.

Potassium

What it does: A lack of potassium has been suggested to aggravate depression.

Where to find it: Bananas. Cooked spinach or broccoli. Sweet potatoes.

Folic acid

What it does: Much of the same. Without enough of it, you may fan the fires of your depression.

Where to find it: Oranges. Leafy greens. Rice.

Omega-3 fatty acids

What it does: An absence of omega-3 in your diet has been linked to sadness.

Where to find it: Walnuts. Seeds (hemp, chia, flax). Brussels sprouts.

Read through that list and pinpoint anything which may be missing in your meals. Then select the associated foods which tickle your tastebuds the loudest and incorporate them into your dishes or snack on them between meals instead. Create a huge smoothie out of these collective ingredients and pretend it's a milkshake. Keep one health food bowl on the table and one on the most eye-level shelf in your fridge, ensuring that you can see them wherever you go. Eat these foods until you are so full that the very idea of sugar makes you feel nauseous.

If you're a picky eater and specific examples make your stomach scrunch, then go ahead and look into supplements instead. And while you are doing that, don't forget to hydrate hydrate hydrate! Keep a bottle of water on your person at all times. A lack of water can kill you faster than almost anything, and your depression will suffer even worse when your brain is drying up and withering away.

"A healthy outside starts from the inside." — Robert Urich

Look, all you need to know is that you are a complex structure made up of chemical compounds, the very sustainable fundamentals of which rely on the fuel you are consuming. As I said yesterday, and I quote, *"if you're spending your days on the couch watching TV whilst eating potato crisps and downing diet cola, you can't reasonably wonder why you're so depressed right now"*. So listen to your mother and eat three balanced meals a day, get plenty of fruit, get plenty of veggies, learn to read food labels, and drink the water. At the same time, slaughter your sugar intake, experiment with cutting out meat/gluten just to see, and feel proud every time you say no to fast-food. Tons of apps monitor your calorie intake and provide nutritional details, so get one of those and eat your way to happiness.

And remember: it's ok to eat whatever you want on weekends because weekend calories don't count. Right?

"Health and cheerfulness naturally beget each other."
— Joseph Addison

And so to recap...

Take a look at your current food selections and be honest about which ones aren't doing your brain any favours. Then use the provided list to select foods you love which also boost the mood. Good mood food!

Start swapping bad foods with better foods and document your progress.

Day 19
Your Spirit

Day 19
Your Spirit

"Imagination is everything. It is the preview of life's coming attractions." — Albert Einstein

Today's discussion is a difficult one. Many of the themes on offer here will be embraced as powerful tools by some, aggressively rejected by others, and ultimately lost on the rest. That said, no matter what your opinion, feel free to roll your eyes at any point, and if it gets to a stage where you want to set this book on fire, don't do that, it would be a waste of money. Rather, stop reading, and move forward to tomorrow. However, even if you are inclined to reject such topics, try your best to bear with me until the very end, just in case something small clicks along the line.

That said, if you are *NOT* of a religious/spiritual nature, go right ahead and skip the next paragraph.

For those of you who do have a connection to a higher power, then I assume that you have already spent many nights calling out to the Universe/God/Life/Fate/The Moon/Whatever to hear your prayers and help you through this painful turmoil. Keep it up! A strong relationship with something greater than yourself will shrink your problems in the bigger plan, providing an understanding that everything is as it's meant to be (even if it's a very testing time indeed). You may even find some peace in these quiet reflections, releasing pleas of help wrapped in gratitude out from yourself, because it's healthy to get the message out of your head and into the control of whatever it is you believe is out there. This practice is not too dissimilar to the other thoughts which I will be touching upon today, but as it stands, you are already at an advantage. You are comfortable in letting your troubles go upwards to wherever they will be received.

"Prayer is not asking. It is a longing of the soul. It is daily admission of one's weakness. It is better in prayer to have a heart without words than words without a heart." — Mahatma Gandhi

Many people have no belief in a higher power, but this does not mean that you cannot access external assistance too, one which is very similar to those who pray within a religious context. There are countless reports of people who have found serenity during yoga postures or martial arts because these roots often come from a place of spiritual understanding. They centre your emotions around an enforced discipline. Not to mention, they also tie in nicely with the physical exercise aspect of your healing! Consider giving them a try if you lack a connection to something outside of yourself.

Another route recommended by just about everyone in the world is that of meditation. Perhaps you are well versed in these techniques, or maybe you consider it to be some useless hippie nonsense, but the evidence is everywhere if you want to read it. Meditation will help you sleep better, it will lower your blood pressure, and it will relax you beneath the fear of anxiety and panic attacks.

"Meditation makes the entire nervous system go into a field of coherence." — Deepak Chopra

Have you tried to meditate but found it too far out of reach? This difficulty is the unfortunate reality of most things. It takes practice to get it right. But whether you scoff at the idea or are willing to give it a go, today is the day to test the waters. Here are a few brief pointers, and while you may not get much out of it, you should get something, even if just the reaffirmation that it's not for you.

Sit upright in a quiet space, ideally for 10 - 30 minutes. If that seems too long of a time, then reduce those numbers to whatever you feel comfortable with, as even a single minute will help. Once you've set yourself up, breathe through your nose for three seconds, hold it for two seconds, then breathe out for your mouth for four seconds. After a few cycles of these, begin to listen to your thoughts as if they were a radio. Don't try to turn the radio off; observe it. Perhaps picture your thoughts as if you are scrolling through a newsfeed. Sometimes a certain thought-post will grab your attention, and you'll forget what you are doing. This is fine. When you remember that you're supposed to be meditating, register that thought's existence, then scroll on. Imagine you are sitting behind yourself, looking into your mind from the outside, watching this information coming and going, never trying to stop it or force it any which way, just enjoying their adorable insanity as they chatter between themselves.

If this doesn't work, try the mantra approach by focusing on one specific thing. It could be an imaginary dot, it could be a particularly funny word, it could be a happy memory, it could be the relaxation of your right foot, it could be the skin of an avocado. You will notice your thoughts will shoot off of this topic in all directions like fireworks. Allow them to do so; it's amusing. But as soon as you notice yourself following one of these escapees, smile, then gently bring your focus back onto that original specific centre point.

"Half an hour's meditation each day is essential, except when you are busy. Then a full hour is needed." — Saint Francis de Sales

If this doesn't work, I highly recommend going online and searching for guided meditation or hypnotic reaffirmation videos on YouTube. Pick one for the most extended length of time that you can fit into your schedule, and listen to it, following its instructions. If you're just getting started, you may find this to be the most beneficial approach. You will be concentrating on something outside of your mind, blasting your brain with a hose of quick suggestions, or distracting your thoughts with gentle wordings which will rock your crazies to sleep. These helped me develop my technique significantly.

If this doesn't work (or even if it does!), try the visualisation approach (or as some of us prefer to call it, "daydreaming"). It may sound silly but do it anyway. Put aside literally a minute a day to imagine a better existence. See yourself winning the lotto, what would be the first thing you'd do with the money? See your next holiday, where are you? You've just won an Oscar, how does your speech go? You've lost some weight, how does that coworker compliment you? Your dream car, what colour is it? See yourself living in prosperity in the mind's eye. Briefly visit the life you want to live and enjoy that feeling as if you already have everything you've ever wanted. Everybody loves you in this world.

If this seems indulgent to you, don't forget that many top athletes swear by this technique as part of their training, watching themselves winning before even participating. So don't laugh it off too soon.

"To dream by night is to escape your life. To dream by day is to make it happen." — Stephen Richards

During this process, it is crucial to maintain full awareness of your breathing. Experiment with the timing. Take long, deep breaths through your nose and into your stomach for 10 seconds. Hold for 10 seconds. Then release out of the mouth. Count them. Picture the total number increasing in your imagination, selecting your favourite font to display it. Breathing is beyond important. Lack of oxygen will kill you faster than the denial of water. Appreciate the action, and you may find yourself getting a little high from it all.

"If you want to conquer the anxiety of life, live in the moment, live in the breath." — Amit Ray, Om Chanting and Meditation

Once you reach a conclusion (even if it's a frustrated *"this doesn't work!"*), end off by giving a brief thank-you to Life itself. Again, this does not have to be a religious declaration, but rather replacing your current emotion with one of gratitude. Maybe life is a nightmare, but I'm confident you can be grateful for, say, your eyes or your hands or your friend or your computer. Anything you can latch onto, anything at all, just for a moment, feel that spark of appreciation. Remember that, yes, in fact, you are still very very lucky in comparison to a large percentage of the world irrespective of your shredded relationship status.

The idea of this exercise is to give your overworked mental cogs a period to chill while lubricating the pathways of inner peace, which (with practice) will make it much easier to access at a moment's notice. When those old familiar thoughts of your ex stab at your vibe, you can use these steps to build a habit which can instantly throw your pain off course. Suppose you've found a mantra which works for you, or you have a go-to happy memory, or you've established a particularly powerful visualisation of success. In these cases, you can replace the ugliness as a default defence mechanism. Register the existence of your upset, then gently push it out the way with a thought you've designed just for this occasion. Then breathe into the thought itself, filling it with oxygen until it thrives.

"Do not spoil what you have by desiring what you have not; remember that what you now have was once among the things you only hoped for." — Epicurus

If you are interested in delving into meditation further, there are countless resources to help you along. Test out online tutorials, free workshops, expensive workshops, books, apps etc. Explore which route works best for you, and spend five minutes before bed performing a peaceful visualisation as it will provide your existence with immeasurable tranquillity.

Finally, if you truly feel the fibres in your body rejecting everything I've just said, there is a little (somewhat detrimental) shortcut method available. Give up, and indulge in some mind-numbing entertainment. Video games, films, TV series, and books are all proven to remove the mind from reality. There are additional healing properties in the power of comedy (especially if you know of a stand-up comedian who is particularly hilarious), so turn off and let the laughter roll. Even fake laughing has reportedly helped people. Try forcing out the stupidest, most ingenuine laugh possible until the silliness amuses you into happiness. But be warned: in excess, these lazier routes can leave you feeling guilty and unfulfilled, which is a negative outcome. That's the opposite of where we're trying to go here. Use media and art sparingly, or use it selectively as a source of inspiration, or don't use it at all.

One final potent trick to get out the mud: if you're ever feeling major despair, shout the words *"ice cream!"* in the angriest meanest voice you can muster. It will lift your mood every time.

"If you have fear of some pain or suffering, you should examine whether there is anything you can do about it. If you can, there is no need to worry about it; if you cannot do anything, then there is also no need to worry." — Dalai Lama

And so to recap...

Today was the problematic conversation about getting out of your brain and focusing on your "energy". Everyone's path will be different. It's up to you to find what works and how to fit it into your daily routine. Prayer? Meditation? Comedy? Weigh up your options and document the best choice for you.

Day 20
You Are The Best Ever

Day 20
You Are The Best Ever

"Wanting to be someone else is a waste of the person you are."
— Marilyn Monroe

The previous three days were so typical to any heartbreak guide that I almost feel embarrassed to have included them. However, their importance should not be overshadowed by their over-usage, as it would have been highly irresponsible of me to ignore their deserved place in this delicate process.

That said, I do hope you forgive me! To make up for it here is something far more fun! Maybe even the most fun day of them all! Go grab your notepad and get ready! Quickly!

"I have an everyday religion that works for me. Love yourself first, and everything else falls into line." — Lucille Ball

We are going to make a list. At the top of an empty page, write the header *100 Reasons Why I Am the Best Ever*. Following that title, you are going to do exactly what you think: write 100 reasons why you are the best ever. I know 100 seems like a excessive number, and I know you could very well feel quite far from the best ever, but don't stress, I'm still talking.

Right now, today, we are going to start with just ten reasons to get the ball bouncing, and then we'll write down the other 90 as they come to you over the next few days (or even weeks). Although let it be known that you could effortlessly write 100 today, no problems, trust me. How do I know this? Because when we're looking at 100 different points, there is no boast too big nor glory too small. Anything will do. Some reasons will inevitably be dumber than others, but each point (no matter how insignificant) will build momentum, and help you connect to the consecutive point much easier.

"You've got to love yourself first. You've got to be okay on your own before you can be okay with somebody else." — Jennifer Lopez

Below are some examples to get you started. Many of these will already apply to you or could be moulded into some description of you. So let's give it a go, shall we?

- I am forever trying to improve myself, which is why I bought this heartbreak book.
- I can cook a killer pasta.
- I am relatively attractive, or so I have been told.
- I know a lot about fish, and I am good with dogs.
- I am better at talking about my feelings than most people.
- I keep my ears clean.
- I don't steal.
- I've watched many films in my time.
- I can mimic the mating call of a lyrebird.
- I have nice hair.
- I earn an acceptable salary, and I am independent.
- I am good at buying birthday gifts.
- I can tap dance.
- I can type really fast.
- I've travelled a fair amount.
- I always cover my mouth when I cough.
- I can pull really funny faces.
- I try to be kind to everyone.
- I'm a good kisser.
- I once met David Hasselhoff.

Think about what your friends would say. What do they like about you? What have you impressed someone with recently? What did the last person compliment you on? What can you do that no one else you know can? What's your party trick? What are your greatest achievements? Think ambition, appearance, professional, sexual, personality, social, intellectual, anything! The more time you spend coming up with these points, the more small details you will notice throughout the coming days, which will remind you of your brilliance. You'll feel that click and think *"that's another factor I can add to my list!"* then do so. Keep adding to it. Keep adding to it. Keep adding to it. Make this part of your routine. And eventually, you will have forced out a 100. Or even 1,000. Go on forever, if you can. And yes, I did once meet David Hasselhoff. He was a nice guy.

"You can't let someone else lower your self-esteem, because that's what it is. Self-esteem. You need to first love yourself before you have anybody else love you." — Winnie Harlow

For extra power, I earnestly recommend that you read your list out loud to yourself in the mirror before you go to bed every night. If it feels silly, good! Feeling silly is better than feeling depressed, no? So that is never an excuse. Go ahead, be loud and say it with confidence because that will be even funnier. And when you go to bed, your dreaming mind will organise these affirmations and file them accordingly. Then who knows? Maybe sooner rather than later, you will actually become the best ever...

"It sounds like a cliché but I also learnt that you're not going to fall for the right person until you really love yourself and feel good about how you are." — Emma Watson

To conclude (and as the saying goes) nobody is perfect. On the flip side of that, however, is that nobody is entirely useless either. No matter how inadequate you currently feel, you could pull enough content out from your bum to fill an entire notebook of reasons why you are the best ever. It could take months, but each case you put forward will elevate your self-opinion ever so slightly, and revive your worthiness of love.

And the best thing about this little game? Is that it should be a lot of fun! If you aren't having fun when you attempt this, you should probably set it aside and try again tomorrow. Because, remember, it is just that. It is all any of this is. A game. And you're playing it right now. So play.

"Oh baby, you should go and love yourself." — Justin Bieber

And so to recap...

Today is nothing but good times as you scribble down anything and everything that makes you so uniquely awesome.
Come up with 10 for now then continue adding to the list for the remainder of this book until you reach 100. No point is too small!

Day 21
Design A Lover

Day 21
Design A Lover

"We waste time looking for the perfect lover, instead of creating the perfect love." — Timothy Oliveira

Did you enjoy yesterday's project? Did you have fun writing your list? Are you having even more fun adding to it as you think of new items? If not, then I am genuinely sorry. If so, however, then I have some excellent news for you...

Today we will be compiling another list! That's right, another list! And there is a good chance that this one will be even more entertaining than the one before! Back to the notebook! Hooray!

Write down the following heading, selecting your preferred gender (or not): *Thank You So Much For My New Boyfriend/Girlfriend/Whatever. I Am So Grateful For Them Because...*

Much like before, beneath this title, you will be writing 100 points, each of which will complete the above sentence, describing your perfect lover precisely. We will be starting with 10 (or more!) today, and then you can slowly add ten more to it each day that passes by, as well as whenever a new factor strikes at your strings. Simples!

"I used to believe in one true soul mate, but not anymore. I believe you can have a few." — Paul Walker

The whole point here is just as it was before: have a blast! Pretend that you are some deity stitching together bits of your desires and moulding them into human form. The perfect human form created just for you.

If you are a bit stuck on getting the pen gliding, look back at Day 4. What were those things your ex did that you couldn't stand? What were the things your ex wasn't? That's what you want. You could even go back to yesterday's list and write down matching qualities which would complement the aspects which you are already offering the world. Easy peasy!

"Having experienced everything you don't want in a partner over time, it starts to narrow down to what you actually do want."
— Jennifer Aniston

Still stuck? Need help? That's why I'm here! Look at the following examples, remembering that there is no trait too small nor too silly to be included.

- They have a cool haircut.
- They smell like candy floss.
- They always wash the dishes.
- They are highly photogenic.
- They kiss super well.
- They love to sleep until late.
- They are ambitious and have a lot of money.
- They love to talk for hours, sometimes just about me.
- They have perfect grammar.
- They enjoy a particular sex act that I dare not write down.
- They have great friends.
- They are very athletic and flexible.
- They are my ideal age.
- They cook a fantastic casserole dish.
- They want to have kids one day.
- They are dedicated to me.
- They have an accent.
- They can do an impressive Elvis Presley impersonation.
- They are not racist.
- They think I am the greatest.

"When you have clarity and commit to manifesting your heart's desire, you will be drawn to those who light you up on every level, and they will be drawn to you." — Annette Vaillancourt, How to Manifest Your Soulmate with Eft: Relationship as a Spiritual Path

Did you notice that we are writing this list in the present tense as if this person already exists and is your dedicated lover? There is a mighty reason behind this, which goes by many names.

Some call it reprogramming or reaffirmations: a method of bluffing your subconscious, tricking it into feeling as if you already have said partner, providing relief as you exude that charming appeal of someone who is in love.

Others call it manifestation: the theory that if we think about something often enough (especially if we pretend it's already in our possession), then it will appear before us in the physical realm much faster.

Others call it voodoo: like a spell you're casting to the Universe or Mother Nature, summoning the ideal partner from the ashes of your ex.

Call it what you want, I don't care, and it doesn't matter. Just follow these instructions even if you feel like you're only humouring me, because what do you have to lose? And once you've written down these factors, repeat them out loud to make sure that the voodoo works. Oops, did I say voodoo? I meant reprogramming!

Seriously though, even if you doubt this step's power, I urge you to set aside what you believe and treat it like a fun game. And by speaking these words out loud, your voice will cement happy vibes into your psyche. Your memory will be up to date. And your active mind will be set on high alert, watching out for that perfect partner as the endless stream of potential candidates pass you every day. So make your order.

"Don't settle for anybody just to have someone. Set your standards. What kind of love do you want to attract? List the qualities you really want in the relationship. Develop those qualities in yourself and you will attract a person who has them." — Louise Hay

If you want to take this to the next level and turn it into something truly insane, then why not adopt these points into creative projects? Draw a little cartoon of each one. Paint a masterpiece which incorporates a few of these points into one scenario. Include an image of yourself in the project by using yesterday's list as inspiration. Write a short story about a possible five-minute exchange between the two of you in the future which sweeps over as many of these aspects as you can fit in. Or, at very least, spend two minutes a day imagining this person before you, then fall in love with them. These exercises are not only fun but will also combat sadness and turn your destructive heartbreak into a worthwhile project.

Once you've reached a point of satisfaction with this task, you should start to realise everything that your ex was not. Perhaps you even let your standards down by being with them? I'm sure they had some marvellous qualities that may pang your chest (and those should be added to your designed lover too), and that's okay to remember. However, to seriously think that your ex was the best-matched person for you, when we live in a world of well over 7.5 billion people, then you are not thinking this through or are preventing your imagination from floating freely. The relationship didn't work for a reason.

Today is an important day; one where you begin to unravel certain imperfections of your ex which weren't compatible with your imperfections. You should slowly be grasping the fundamental truth: you deserve better things. Some of the evilest humans in history found love, and you are not as bad as them. You deserve love much more than they did. You deserve a love that works. You deserve love from a person who ticks every one of the boxes you just created. And what's more, statistically speaking, they exist and are probably out there looking for you right now.

"Personally, I think if a woman hasn't met the right man by the time she's 24, she may be lucky." — Oprah

Because here's the thing, everyone is looking for different factors in a lover. No two people would write the same list as you just did. So while this magical person you have designed from thin air may seem like some unattainable, nonexistent entity who would never fall for someone like you... stop. And think again. Considering all the people on the planet with the infinitely complex variations of personalities that occur, there are probably a million of them who would fit your criteria precisely. They will also come with a bunch of flaws you didn't even consider, but don't worry about that just yet.

What's more, all they want is what anybody wants. Someone who will appreciate them for their unique qualities. And you could be that for them. Which is why, when you meet someone new, you are now armed with a specific list of requirements, ensuring that your next lover (no matter how long they may take to find you) will be an upgrade, just so long as you don't settle.

Hear my words: unless you die soon, you will heal one day, and you will fall in love again (if you are open to it). It is inevitable because that's how human are wired. We are all searching for companionship, a place to store our loneliness out of sight. It may take time, but when it happens, remember what I said today, and then transfer me £100 via Paypal as a thank you.

"Don't look for a soul mate. Make one, out of the complex fabric of the human being already with you. Instructions are never included. They vary with the strength of your ability to see, the measure of your selective blindness, the limits of your mercy, and the intensity of your desire." — Vera Nazarian; The Perpetual Calendar of Inspiration

And so to recap...

Today was kind of like yesterday, except instead of pulling good qualities about yourself outward, you are pulling qualities of your perfect lover inward. Write ten today, keep going until you reach 100 in total, and have fun!

Day 22
Service

Day 22
Service

"Service to others is the rent you pay for your room here on earth."
— Muhammad Ali

Now that we've been selfishly touching on ourselves for the longest reasonable time, the day has come where we must turn this attention and energy outwards. Get ready to unleash one of the most powerful moves you can perform, turning your life into something worthwhile and meaningful. And that is... to help other people.

"It is literally true that you can succeed best and quickest by helping others to succeed." — Napoleon Hill

Since the dawn of deep thought, there have been complex philosophical debates which question whether a selfless act exists. Of course, when a person appears to be a great asset to their community by lending a helping hand, they are rightfully lauded as an admirable person. However, they are still carrying out these acts of kindness because they enjoy it.

More often than not, humans who possess this seemingly natural supportive drive are only doing so because they've discovered a trigger, one which is fundamental to our very survival, embedded down within our instinctive genetic makeup. I'm not attempting to devalue the act of compassion, but the fact is when you help someone, your brain unleashes a bucket-ton of dopamine, serotonin, and oxytocin all over your neurons, blasting happiness to every corner of your being. That's why you get that warm and fuzzy feeling when you've done a good deed. It has evolved that way because helping our fellow humans ensures our species' existence continues to thrive and survive, and survival is the #1 priority of all instincts in the first place.

"The best way to not feel hopeless is to get up and do something. Don't wait for good things to happen to you. If you go out and make some good things happen, you will fill the world with hope, you will fill yourself with hope." — Barack Obama

If the previous paragraph encourages your altruistic impulses or puts you off the philanthropic concept because now it's ruined as yet another act of selfishness... don't think about it. Avoid getting yourself tangled in the details and do your part in making the world a nicer place to live. There is no downside to this, it has very little chance of going wrong, and according to everyone (including yourself), you will seem like a better person because of it. And you know why? Because you *will* be a better person because of it, by the very definition of the term.

"You have not lived today until you have done something for someone who can never repay you." — John Bunyan

There are hundreds of ways to achieve this, but it's mainly about developing a keen awareness and consideration for all people (and animals and environmental issues) who require assistance. And then you assist them. For some, this will come naturally. For others, not so much. But regardless of your current level of benevolence, it's time to start actively seeking out ways to heal the world. Take action then write them down in your diary as your little rewarding pat on the back. Give the love you don't have, and then you shall have it.

"The best cure for weariness is the challenge of helping someone who is even more tired. One of the great ironies of life is this: he or she who serves almost always benefits more than he or she who is served."
— Gordon B. Hinckley; Standing for Something

Here is a quick list of good deeds and general positive vibrations you can start implementing into your daily routine right now:

- Give spare change to the homeless.
- Give up your seat for the elderly.
- Help a stranger carry a box or luggage down the stairs.
- Smile at random people on the street (without being creepy).
- Recycle.
- Always say *please* and *thank you*.
- Volunteer at an animal shelter or a soup kitchen or a children's hospital.
- Listen to a friend who is having relationship troubles right now, and fight the urge to talk about yourself.
- Try to email a different friend almost every day and express gratitude for the role they've played in your life.
- Don't litter.
- Always give credit when credit is due.
- Clean the toilet after use, if it warrants it.
- Open the door for people.
- Save paper and don't print out anything you don't need to.
- Compliment people as often as you can.
- Offer coffee to others when you make your own.
- Just be nice.

"I have found that among its other benefits, giving liberates the soul of the giver." — Maya Angelou

For a lot of these examples, the benefits are twofold. Firstly, you will (more often than not) instantaneously receive a thankful response, which should strengthen your general relationship with the human race whilst also lifting your spirits. And secondly, you might (somewhat embarrassingly) realise how pathetic your problems were in the greater scheme of troubles. Your issues may shrink as you remember that you are not the only person in the world who is suffering. The whole world is suffering, and what's more, some are suffering far worse than you have ever suffered before. Your heartbreak isn't in the top 100 bad things that could happen to you. Not even close.

"The best way to find yourself is to lose yourself in the service of others." — Mahatma Gandhi

I want to end today off with a little bonus level which even the most charitable of individuals seem to trip over. Naturally, when you perform an action which helps someone else, often your first reaction is to pull out your phone and tell the world what a great person you are with a smug selfie like a celebratory rub on the head. This act dilutes the genuine generosity into a puddle of congratulatory boasting rights, and the ever-unobtainable selfless act moves even further away. It also makes you look like a bloated bubble of arrogance, and nobody likes those. Instead, do your best not to tell anyone about your good deeds. Maybe you won't get any high-fives, but inside of your body, you'll have this elated secret just between you and yourself that you did the right thing for the right reasons. And that is far more powerful and special.

"At the end of life we will not be judged by how many diplomas we have received, how much money we have made, how many great things we have done. We will be judged by 'I was hungry, and you gave me something to eat, I was naked and you clothed me. I was homeless, and you took me in.'" — Mother Teresa

For the record: this is the fastest way known to humans to feel better and to heal your broken heart, guaranteed. Just look at all the quotes I've posted above. Those are some big names who know what they are saying. Do not let this advice pass you. Take some initiative and test it out for yourself.

"And in the end, the love you take is equal to the love you make."
— The Beatles, The End

And so to recap...

Today was all about building an awareness of the world around you and finding ways to improve it.
Using the provided list as guidance, write down some small ways in which you could help people or your surrounding environment, then make a plan to do so over the coming days.

Day 23
Reevaluation Day

Day 23
Reevaluation Day

"I don't have a photograph, but you can have my footprints. They're upstairs in my socks." — Groucho Marx

Well, would you look at that! Another week has passed! And so, as before, let us take some time to reflect on how far you've come, as well as granting some additional attention to the days you feel you could have done better.

Have you kept the communication lines shut between you and your ex? No contact at all? Or (if there were some pressing issues) at least to the very bare minimum, avoiding any realms of unnecessary emotional fallbacks and arguments? I hope so, because each time you slip up, you are taking a major step backwards. It's one of the most critical parts of this book for a reason. If you can't hold this aspect together, much of this program will be lost. That said, whether you've failed or succeeded, the end of our journey is coming, so please hang on and cut them off, rereading Day 5 if needs be.

Related: please don't forget to keep writing down everything you want to say to them on paper (without saying anything to them at all), as this is still important for later.

Have you been hanging out with different friends and enjoying your reintroduction into the world of socialising without your ex? Do you have next week's meet up already planned in place? If not, pick up that phone.

Speaking of socialising, have you managed to keep your real life and social media presence as one of (perhaps even fake) optimism? Not a place to fish for sympathy? Did you decide to meet a professional and follow through? Have you minimised any intoxicated mistakes? Have you managed to dodge any desperate rebounding? Take a moment to answer these questions honestly, and keep an eye on these factors.

Remember: the more you put in, the more you get out.

"Do you want to know who you are? Don't ask. Act! Action will delineate and define you." — Thomas Jefferson

By now, your appearance should be measurably different, your bedroom should look like a new place, and your house should have started to become a much cleaner environment. Please spend some time today looking over those parts of your recovery and finding new, fun ways to alter their presentation even further. Get crazy with it.

Last week, we discussed the standard but imperative procedure of getting some physical activity into your life, eating a little healthier, and finding a way to get out of your head (whether it be via meditation or some other external distraction). Admittedly, these aren't the most exciting or original of ideas. Still, they will speed up your recovery time dramatically whilst blessing your racing mind with moments of peace, clarity, and a sensation of satisfaction. Do not overlook these suggestions, as many people find them to be the most effective surge forward and they are the most common suggestions for a reason.

We also recently started writing two lists. One of these detailed the amazingness of you and the other one described the perfect lover who you built like a character from the Sims. By today you should have around 30 - 40 points per each list, and so if you're behind, put some time aside right now to revisit this exercise (Days 20 and 21). And remember to have as much fun as possible with it!

"When you go through heartbreak, you just do the things that get you by. Eventually, you realise it's about making the most of life."
— Britney Spears

Yesterday, we spoke about the magic of helping the world around us. Hopefully, due to my brilliantly eloquent writing skills, you should readily understand why this method can evaporate the selfish upset inside of you, and turn it around into an act which benefits everything outside of your skull. Have you come up with any ideas on how to do so yet? Have you already started? If not, start now! Today!

And that's how far we've come, which is a lot of stuff! Take note in your diary of the aspects you feel you are excelling at, and give yourself a handshake. Then write down the elements where you think you could focus more attention. Prioritise those bits that are falling behind, trying your best to sort out a plan today.

"Of course motivation is not permanent. But then, neither is bathing; but it is something you should do on a regular basis." — Zig Ziglar, Raising Positive Kids in a Negative World

Finally, let's do that emotional ladder thing again! It's good to get into the practice of registering your feelings when they are in a negative space and then stop. And then breathe. And then come to this list and work out how to take the next step upwards. Visit this ladder as often as possible, starting from now. Locate the emotion which you think best describes your current insides, then do your best to climb up one point. Then another and another, as high as possible.

The Emotional Ladder

1. Liberation!
2. Hopefulness and Excitement
3. Relief and Satisfaction
4. Boredom
5. Lost Confusion
6. Irritation, Frustration, and Impatience
7. Sadness, Loneliness, and Longing
8. Doubtfulness and Discouragement
9. Furious Anger
10. Vengeful Hatred
11. Destructive Hatred
12. Jealousy

13. Fearful Anxiety
14. Unlovable Worthlessness
15. Utter Devastation and Depression

"It's not the load that breaks you down, it's the way you carry it."
— Lou Holtz

We are gradually nearing the end of our journey, and so this final week is going to be mostly focusing on quick ninja tricks you can perform for potent and immediate relief. Some of these ideas will seem a little difficult or daunting, but as we're so close to the finish line, we've got to hit this hole with everything we've got. Get ready for that, and we'll speak tomorrow, you lovely creature, you.

*"The only thing standing between you and your goal is the bulls**t story you keep telling yourself as to why you can't achieve it."*
— Jordan Belfort

And so to recap...

Today was another reevaluation day, giving you a break to look back over the past weeks and make a note of what requires further attention.
What's going well? What can you do to tighten up these wonky bits before moving forward? Write these answers down and then make a plan!

Day 24
Success Is The Best Revenge

Day 24
Success Is The Best Revenge

"Opportunities are usually disguised as hard work, so most people don't recognise them." — Ann Landers

Let's pause and talk about revenge for a second. As any professional will tell you, revenge is not the healthiest objective. It is essentially the same as looking fiercely over your shoulder, spitting backwards towards a relationship that once was. And when you're facing backwards, how are you supposed to move forward?

That said, I am not a newcomer to this game. I am well aware that many people reading this book are swimming with the desire to make an ex regret ever leaving them, no matter who pulled the plug. I know this because that's how I was.

"I'm a fighter. I believe in the eye-for-an-eye business. I'm no cheek turner. I got no respect for a man who won't hit back. You kill my dog, you better hide your cat." — Muhammad Ali

The good news here is that, whatever your intentions, much of this book will have indirectly achieved some degree of constructive revenge already. If the social vine has been trickling information to them (and it always does), your ex should be aware how you're sporting a brand new style as your general outlook appears to be one of remarkable progress. They probably don't particularly enjoy that.

"The best revenge is massive success." — Frank Sinatra

Today we are going to take this approach one step further, and even if your honourable motivation is not one of vengeance, the content on offer here is (above all else) a healthy system to further your recovery.

If that bothers someone else, then tough. On the flip side, if inflicting some sinister discomfort of repentance into your ex sounds like fun to you, then you can turn this towards that direction too. It is the most excellent method of inflicting revenge known to man.

So how do you do it? By working really, really hard. Drive yourself to finish a major project (or two or more), and reap all the yummy returns such an undertaking can provide. You will fill your hours, you will be distracted from your pain, and you will dine on the refined pleasure that only these accomplishments can generate. Depending on your chosen project, it could also come with various other rewards, in terms of finances, social prestige, or even a fitness orientated result. And finally, the inadequacy that your ex will feel beneath your rising success will merely seem like a happy side effect, one you can pretend you didn't even notice.

"Revenge, the sweetest morsel to the mouth that ever was cooked in hell." — Walter Scott, The Heart of Mid-Lothian

A casual way to start this process is to calculate how much time you are saving by not being in a relationship right now. Add up the minutes of your past partnership by including the meals together, the going out, the conversations (or arguments), hanging with their friends, visiting their parents, and whatever else you can calculate. Once you have a ballpark figure of how much weekly free time you have gained as a single person, you now know how much time you can dedicate to the more important stuff. Perhaps even the things your ex wasn't keen on you doing before.

If you are initially unsure about what your project should be, try immersing yourself in your professional life. Say yes to things. Take on more challenging tasks. Get involved with activities after work. Seek a collaborative project for additional responsibility. Freelance for extra money. Arrive at your work early each day to shift your mindset into work mode, then dedicate this time to your projects. Stay later at your job to do the same. You will enjoy the quiet time, not to mention that the facilities will be all yours outside of work hours and it will impress to your boss. If this all sounds like your worst nightmare, apply these same principles to finding a new job.

"When someone is mean to me, I just make them a victim in my next book." — Mary Higgins Clark

You may often find that your weekends are your loneliest point, in which case you need to find a hobby immediately (or rekindle an old one). If you already have a hobby that you adore, this is now your priority. Work on it with fury. If you do not have one, then finding one is your priority. Didn't you have that cool idea once upon a time? Maybe you should finally pursue that? Have you ever knitted a jersey? Tried indoor rock climbing? Painted a post-modernist masterpiece? Trained for a marathon? Written a short story? Starred in a play? Mastered the harp? Sculpted a candle? Planted a garden? Joined a quiz team? The possibilities are endless, and even if you try one and hate it, do not worry! Throw it aside and attempt another one. Distractions. That is what you are looking for here. Drown yourself in them.

I mean, don't literally drown yourself in them, and always stop if you feel yourself burning out. Only bite off what you can digest. Don't prioritise this over your health. You are no good to me dead.

"Falling in love is awesome, but I'm never drawn to happy songs per se, so whenever you sit down to write a heartbreak song and you're happily in love, it's like, 'OK, now I have to go back to a sad place to get something good.'" — Miranda Lambert

You can take this concept one step deeper into the oft-overlooked potential within your darkness. If you think about the art world, what is the dominant inspiration that runs throughout? Love and heartbreak. One of which you are feeling right now, as inarguably the most powerful emotion a human being can harbour. That is why so many of the most significant art pieces ever made came from the same anguish you hold inside of you at this very moment. If you can find a way to smash creativity through this special window available to you at this very moment, what comes out the other side may be of a uniquely potent form of suffering. Not everyone has current access to this place, yet millions will wholeheartedly relate to it. Even if you are not an artist, give it a go. Capitalise on your unfortunate situation. Turn it into something valuable.

"A letdown is worth a few songs. A heartbreak is worth a few albums."
— Taylor Swift

Truth be told, the initially proposed revenge angle was more of an alluring camouflage, as the advantages of this scheme extend far beyond something so frivolous. Having a creative project or a pressing responsibility grants you a purpose—a reason to get up in the morning, with momentum to run through the day. The harder you work, the faster time goes, the less you will think. And once you have finished a project, you may even (dare I say it) be extremely thankful for the heartbreak that happened in the first place. Because now you have this artistic thing or a bigger paycheque, born out of an intense passion which would not exist otherwise.

"We should forgive our enemies, but not before they are hanged"
— Heinrich Heine

And what if… just what if… it turns into something much bigger? What if it really sells? What if you get promoted? What if you become rich and revered and famous and everything? Nothing, and I mean nothing, will make your ex want you back more. And nothing will make you want your ex back less.

On a personal note: I wrote a book to exploit my turmoil. You're busy reading it right now.

"Life is sometimes hard. Things go wrong, in life and in love and in business and in friendship and in health and in all other ways that life can go wrong. And when things get tough, this is what you should do: make good art." — Neil Gaiman

And so to recap...

Today was all about finding new ways to throw yourself into a project, whether it be your job, a hobby, or a creative idea. Come up with a list of potential avenues, pick one or two which appeals to you the most, and then calculate the first step. How would that go?

Day 25
Terrorise Yourself

Day 25
Terrorise Yourself

"It's okay to be scared. Being scared means you're about to do something really, really brave." — Mandy Hale, The Single Woman: Life, Love, and a Dash of Sass

Do you still have days when the sharp stabs of loneliness make your heart thud without rhythm? Does your stomach perform washing machine churns as your brain sends signals of self-doubt through your veins? Never fear! For there is a way to find immediate relief from this pain whenever it comes along. And that way is to *always* live in fear! What could go wrong?

We have been training together for a while now. I feel like you are finally ready for this distinctive finisher move which will displace all of your negative emotion, shoving the turbulence aside and directing every fibre of your energy into a new realm of trouble. And that is to freak yourself out completely.

"Life begins at the end of your comfort zone." — Neale Donald Walsch

The concept is so simple, that even as you read these words, you will know that I am speaking the truth. If you purposely induce anxiety towards something externally scary, you will not be thinking about your ex nor will your feelings of misery even be relevant at that time. Your adrenaline will take the wheel, you will regret ever deciding to prod said fear, and you'll curse my name in the process. But if you are currently suffering from a severe case of the heartaches, this will be one heck of a fast-track way through because it works out-of-the-box without delay.

Here are some examples, and I want you to take a moment to

contemplate each one as if you are already participating in that action. Even this visualisation practice could give you a taste of what I mean.

- Book a solo holiday to a country where you don't speak the language.
- Talk to a stranger in a bar.
- Book a skydiving session.
- Sign up to do a photoshoot.
- Sing karaoke in front of a room full of strangers.
- Find a snake farm and hold a few of these creatures.
- Join an open mic poetry session.
- Scuba dive in murky waters.
- Attend a loud raucous party where you don't know anyone.
- Locate the highest point of altitude in your city, then climb to the top of it while looking down all the way.

"Thinking will not overcome fear but action will." — W. Clement Stone

Do any of these examples scare the hell out of you? Do any of these examples sound like something you are curious to try? Do any of these examples give you another idea? What's your greatest fear? Then you've got it. Sign up right now. Right. Now. I guarantee you that even in the planning and anticipating of these events, the dread will devour your thoughts and the memory of your ex will struggle to take control away from the terror you have just inflicted upon yourself. Maybe there will be fleeting moments where your ex's name will scream in your head once again, but when you recall that terrifying event you agreed to participate in, your thoughts will quickly turn back, far too preoccupied with nerves and excitement to even bother with the idea of someone else. It is an instant relief, whenever you want it, all yours, my gift to you.

If you reckon that you are in the worst place you could imagine, book a shark cage diving course off the shores of South Africa, and you will realise that you were very wrong.

"It's good to feel stupid sometimes and do things that are out of your comfort zone." — *Mary-Louise Parker*

What's more, after you have completed each task, you will come out of it with an elevated sense of conquering something horrifying, and like many before, you may even become quite addicted to the feeling of this extreme fear. And on you will go, each portion of dread creating another stepping stone away from where you are. Furthermore, whenever your mind wanders into darker regions, you can get into the habit of recalling these insane memories, and this intense recollection will provide immediate alleviation. Plus, your photos will look great!

"Decide that you want it more than you are afraid of it."
— *Anonymous*

For the record (and to let you know that I'm not playing games here merely to torture you) I took this step very seriously. I participated in open mic poetry, I got a facial piercing, and I modelled for a photoshoot, all of which freaked me out to varying degrees. But my pride and joy was when I got suspended. For those who don't know what that means, it goes like this: two large meat hooks were shoved into my shoulders which lifted me into the sky by my skin. A pretty drastic move, for sure, but I was in a drastic place, and the point stands strong. Do you think I was heartbroken when they pierced a considerable chunk of my flesh? How many times do you think my ex crossed my mind whilst I was impaled in the air, adrenaline pumping throughout my system and blissful pain replacing every single cell of my body? I'll give you a hint: none. For in those moments (as well as the moments leading up to it), I was free of everything negative, reaching new levels of self-discovery, which stuck with me for days afterwards. In some ways, it still hasn't entirely left me.

In conclusion, this is the tried-and-tested greatest method of escaping your current mental space, and from your newfound platform of fear, it is much easier to structure a permanent escape route. If you are in a pressing rut which feels like a dead-end and is in dire need of a dramatic kickstart, then here is your motorbike. Do not just pass this day by as if it's some joke. If you genuinely need help, then this is the help you are asking for. Use it.

"Expose yourself to your deepest fear; after that, fear has no power, and the fear of freedom shrinks and vanishes. You are free."
— Jim Morrison

And so to recap...

Today we looked at a powerful move where you can dominate any emotion by intentionally shoving your soul full of fear. Make a list of ideas which terrify you and research how you would go about pursuing them. Even if you don't follow through, just the planning alone may be enough to scare the heartbreak right out!

Day 26
Special Level Up

Day 26
Special Level Up

"Darkness cannot drive out darkness; only light can do that. Hate cannot drive out hate; only love can do that."
— Martin Luther King, Jr.

Continuing to break out the big guns, today we are going to look at a different heavy-duty move of relief that you can perform immediately. There is a unique element of power associated with this suggestion, and it will add yet another durable stitch to your wound (even if it may feel like you're fixing things from the opposite angle).

Putting your ex aside for a moment, is there anyone else in your life that you currently dislike? A person with who you recently argued? Someone you've held a grudge against since the dawn of time? A different ex with who you've never made amends? A person you loathe with all of your heart and soul with an infuriating passion? A person you could never imagine speaking to again? Now is the time to get in contact with them, and bury that animosity once and for all.

"To be wronged is nothing, unless you continue to remember it."
— Confucius

I know this step may seem terrifying and annoyingly irrelevant to the primary objective, but there is a strong reason behind it. It shifts the focus from your heartbreaker onto someone else who has caused you grief, and then by allowing this other person back into your life, you will teach yourself how to heal stale afflictions. In turn, this may have a domino effect where you find yourself enjoying the alleviation of letting the pain go. And above even this, it is an exercise in practising forgiveness, of growing up emotionally as a person, of being the bigger human, and of calculating the finer details involved in setting something free.

Ok, but just quickly, what if you're the nicest person in the world? What if you have no one that you dislike or dislikes you? In that highly unlikely case, then you're just going to have to dig deep and recall some previous situation that you could have handled better, no matter how insignificant it may seem now. And then repair the past by patching it up. That said, I'm relatively convinced that (no matter who you are) there is someone on your mind right now. Someone you have bad vibes with which you could address. Be honest with yourself.

"It is the highest form of self-respect to admit our errors and mistakes and make amends for them. To make a mistake is only an error in judgment, but to adhere to it when it is discovered shows infirmity of character." — Dale Turner

Even if you don't feel ready for it, you can surely comprehend that this previous conflict serves no purpose to you. And as your heart currently suffers a much larger assault, what does this other argument even mean in comparison? Let's rather alleviate some of this burden you're carrying. Lighten the load. Because whatever this person did, it's not worth wasting any more of your brain space on it.

The best way to look at it is like this: it's not up to you to judge whether someone is terrible or deserves hostility or not. You are not the authority on forgiveness. By hanging onto resentment towards a person, it means nothing to anyone except for you. You are carrying a negative emotion for this human, which will only serve to hurt your insides, and no one else's. If it makes it any easier, think of them as a tool. By opening the paths of communication and extending a hand of compassion, it is for your benefit and healing. Not theirs.

"Always forgive your enemies; nothing annoys them so much." — Oscar Wilde

What follows may vary. You could be pleased to discover that this select person has wanted to rebuild this bridge themselves, and a new friendship could be rekindled from an old one, even stronger than before. They could also turn into yet another ear helping to unravel the mystery of your heartache. Or perhaps they will be dismissive or rude or non-responsive, in which case, don't entertain it. Let it fall into the past once again with your head held up high, proud that you gave it a go and were ultimately the better party in this specific exchange.

Do I need to remind you that this is a game? And like any game, it's all about practising your moves, such as forgiveness and discarding unwanted rivalry, killing your enemies with kindness. Perhaps you'll even adore this process so much, that you'll take it a step further by writing a list of everyone you've ever harmed or upset in your life then making peace, ticking them off one by one. And eventually, you may develop a sixth sense to sidestep conflict before it spirals out of control. As this goes on, you will be collecting up game points, improving your score, growing as a person, and starting your new life by upcycling turbulence into turbo-boosters. *Pew!*

"That's a spiritual lifestyle, being willing to admit that you don't know everything and that you were wrong about some things. It's about making a list of all the people you've harmed, either emotionally or physically or financially, and going back and making amends. That's a spiritual lifestyle. It's not a fluffy ethereal concept."
— Anthony Kiedis

And so to recap...

Today's benefits were two-fold. We practised the art of forgiveness, and we focused upon separate matters which are similar to your current experience without being directly related. Write a list of people you are not on good terms with, and then make amends with as many as you can stomach (even if just one).

Day 27
Research Further

Day 27
Research Further

"I went to a bookstore and asked the saleswoman, 'Where's the self-help section?' She said if she told me, it would defeat the purpose." — George Carlin

We are incredibly close to reaching the end of your month now, and so it is my duty to ensure that any gifts this book may have bestowed upon you, stay with you. In that way, we can metaphorically hold hands forever. Doesn't that sound lovely?

You see, the risk with writing any book like this is that I have the responsibility to speak as generally as possible. Only in that way, can I be inclusive to all types of heartbreaks and current walks of healing. What this ultimately means, however, is that not everything I've offered will stick for every single person, and that's fine, because we are individuals. They tell me it's a good thing.

"All our knowledge has its origin in our perceptions." — Leonardo da Vinci

Today's task is simple and tailored perfectly to you. It is important because I won't be around for much longer, and you've got to start taking control of this beast on your own.

Alright, so flip back through your notebook or this book, and then locate the days you thought were an absolute waste of time, writing them down. Once you've done this, repeat the process, except this time, note which days you felt connected to you and were the most beneficial. If you are so inclined, place each day in order from best to worst, or assign each day points for how effective they were, whatever you want. Your intention here is to determine the steps of this journey which resonated loudest within your circumstance. Or perhaps you don't even need to think about it. Perhaps you remember those pages clearly.

"Let him who would move the world first move himself." — Socrates

Done? If so, you should now be able to easily identify at least three days which vibrated most excitedly within your system. These were the days that meant something to you. These were the days you enjoyed the most. These were the days you were good at.

Once you know what those are, the best plan would be to go back and reread them. And then, exploit those chapters for all they're worth. Pump your strength into those specific attacks by discovering new ways in which you can constructively activate them every single day. These are your specialities, your priorities, your superpowers.

To help you get started, here is a quick list of ideas to approach each day productively. Obviously, these are very loose examples, and you would need to be far more specific when it comes to your own life, but hopefully, they should spur on some direction. Locate your days below, and get those cogs turning.

Day 1

Really? Honestly, this isn't the best choice of day for anyone. However, if you're adamant, you could research the topic of sad art and become the authority on the bleakest films/books ever made? Maybe turn your pessimism into a stand-up comedy routine? Or look out for clinical trials that need tears? Or studies that need someone who sleeps a lot? I'd prefer it if you chose something else.

Day 2

This is a bit of a general day to choose but could indicate that you are a person of action, who likes to make a plan and then follow it through. You should write a list of definite short-term/mid-term/long-term goals, evaluate them daily, and then stick to them. Concentrate on organising your time better and researching methods to accelerate your productivity. Try reading *Getting Things Done: The Art of Stress-Free Productivity* by David Allen, and *The 4-Hour Workweek* by Timothy Ferriss.

Day 3

Those who choose an Emotional Ladder day are probably more in tune with their emotions and like to set achievable short-term goals instead of diving into anything too dramatic. Keep an emotions diary, and continue to pursue the maximum awareness of your feelings. Try reading *The Happiness Trap: How to Stop Struggling and Start Living: A Guide to ACT* by Russ Harris, or *The Power of Now: A Guide to Spiritual Enlightenment* by Eckhart Tolle.

Day 4

Make art! Whether illustrative or narrative or via poetic ramblings, you probably have an enthusiasm for bringing your thoughts and emotions into the outside world and crafting them into creative masterpieces. Pick your preferred medium of expression and locate online tutorials which will better improve your chosen skill. Do yourself a favour and seek out Neil Gaiman's speech at the Philadelphia's University of the Arts, usually titled *Make Good Art*, it might change your life, as it did mine. Also try reading *Art and Fear: Observations on the Perils (and Rewards) of Artmaking* by David Bayles and Ted Orland, or *The Artist's Way: A Spiritual Path to Higher Creativity* by Julia Cameron.

Day 5

Use this day as inspiration to get rid off all the toxic people in your life. Go through your social media feeds and regular emails, and remove any individual who is poisoning your happy vibes. Analyse and grade every human connection you have from day-to-day, and streamline these interactions to only include ones who bring you a level of joy at all times possible. Try reading *Emotional Vampires: Dealing with People Who Drain You Dry* by Albert J. Bernstein, and

People Can't Drive You Crazy if You Don't Give Them the Keys by Mike Bechtle.

Day 6

Ah, a social insect. You should see your friends as often as possible, go out more, have fun, and find strength in their support. Practice your skills at being a better conversationalist or storyteller, and research how to gauge people's body language. Become more socially aware of your surroundings, and reap the benefits of friendly love that only other human beings can provide. Try reading *How to Win Friends and Influence People* by Dale Carnegie, *How to Talk to Anyone: 92 Little Tricks for Big Success in Relationships* by Leil Lowndes, and *What Every Body is Saying: An Ex-FBI Agent's Guide to Speed-Reading People* by Joe Navarro and Marvin Karlins.

Day 7

Keep speaking to professionals and following their advice. Some people stay in therapy their whole lives, not because they are basket cases, but because they want to keep their heads as clean and as tight as possible while they tackle their daily tasks. Chat with other people about their therapy battles and successes. These are often the sturdiest characters who have dedicated the much needed time to study themselves. Try reading *Existential Psychotherapy* and *Love's Executioner: & Other Tales of Psychotherapy*, both by Irvin D. Yalom.

Day 8

Abstaining from mind-altering substances seems like a good idea for you. Stick with it. Research more about addiction and toy with the idea of going to AA/NA meetings, hopefully quitting all drugs and alcohol if possible. Try reading *Twelve Steps and Twelve Traditions* by Alcoholics Anonymous, *Allen Carr's Easy Way to Control Alcohol* by Allen Carr, and *Recovery: Freedom from Our Addictions* by Russell Brand.

Day 9
Please see Day 3.

Day 10
Be very picky about who you grant intimacy to while seeking exciting dating options from any viable platform. Test out new online dating tools, refine your bio, upload better photos, and turn your profile into a masterpiece. Ask your friends for help with that. Attend as many single social groups you can find. Try reading *Models: Attract Women Through Honesty* by Mark Manson (if you like girls) or *Get the Guy: Learn Secrets of the Male Mind to Find the Man You Want and the Love You Deserve* by Matthew Hussey (if you like boys) or both (if you like both).

Day 11
As is the ever-changing fashion of fashion, the only way to keep up-to-date on trends of a stylistic nature is by going old-school. Read fashion magazines and blogs while studying celebrities and those around you whose taste you envy, ultimately progressing your external appearance along as one perpetual artistic evolution. Become an icon.

Day 12
Much like the day before, your room and entire house should be one constant development, an unstoppable art project forever in motion. Try reading *Clear Your Clutter with Feng Shui* by Karen Kingston, and keep an eye on the website Nifty (via Buzzfeed).

Day 13
Clean your house more! Clean for an hour! Clean for as long as you like! Clean other people's homes if it helps! Maybe even get paid to do so! Try reading *Clean House Clean Planet* by Karen Logan, and *The Cleaning Bible: Kim and Aggie's Complete Guide to Modern Household Management* by Kim Woodburn and Aggie MacKenzie.

Day 14

Keep working on your schedule, searching for holes, and sharpening the process every day, until you pass everyone else in a blur. At the same time, keep in mind that you are only learning the rules to break them properly, so occasionally do something crazy, compiling a list of fun activities and randomly picking one out of a hat. Also, say yes to (almost) everything! Try reading *Getting Things Done: The Art of Stress-Free Productivity* by David Allen, and *Eat That Frog!: 21 Great Ways to Stop Procrastinating and Get More Done in Less Time* by Brian Tracy. However, I refuse to provide a book example about impulse action because planning to be more spontaneous is a contradiction.

Day 15

As a strict rule, do one thing every day which makes you happy. Perform split-second decisions and take responsibility for it later, just don't tell anyone I told you to do that. Try reading *The Gifts of Imperfection: Let Go of Who You Think You're Supposed to Be and Embrace Who You Are* by Brené Brown, and *Self-Compassion: The Proven Power of Being Kind to Yourself* by Kristin Neff.

Day 16

Please see Day 3.

Day 17

Time to push that body forward as hard as possible! If you haven't already joined a gym, then join a gym. Get a professional trainer and design a gruelling workout plan which sticks. Run as far as you can. Run far far away. Try reading *The 4-Hour Body: An Uncommon Guide to Rapid Fat-Loss, Incredible Sex, and Becoming Superhuman* by Timothy Ferriss, and *Strength Training Anatomy* by Frédéric Delavier.

Day 18

Download every app available that keeps track of your diet. Build a meal plan which works for you, incorporating nothing but goodness and health into your digestive system. Learn what your body needs to function, and make sure you get that every day. Try reading *Lean in 15 - The Shift Plan: 15 Minute Meals and Workouts to Keep You Lean and Healthy* by Joe Wicks, *Why We Get Fat: And What to Do About It* by Gary Taubes, and *The Eat-Clean Diet Recharged!: Lasting Fat Loss That's Better Than Ever!* by Tosca Reno.

Day 19

Assuming you found value in the meditation side of Day 19, continue your daily practice, watching videos to guide your technique, attending sessions in your area, and consider other spiritualistic physical activities such as yoga or martial arts. Read *10% Happier: How I Tamed the Voice in My Head, Reduced Stress Without Losing My Edge, and Found Self-Help That Actually Works* by Dan Harris, and *Wherever You Go, There You Are: Mindfulness Meditation in Everyday Life* by Jon Kabat-Zinn. Otherwise, set aside a *maximum* of a few hours a week to do absolutely nothing except for watching rubbish TV or playing video games (but rather read a book).

Day 20

Keep writing that list about your brilliance! See if you can get to a 1,000 entries! 10,000! A MILLION! Illustrate your favourite ones no matter what your level of drawing skills. Turn it into a comic or a script about your superhero alter ego, just like that. Read *Love Yourself Like Your Life Depends on It* by Kamal Ravikant, and *Choose Yourself: Be Happy, Make Millions, Live the Dream* by James Altucher.

Day 21

Much like the above Day 20 suggestions, keep this list going too! Write a billion details about your perfect lover, and then turn it into an elaborate art project (like a series of paintings or a surrealistic novel or a fully functional robot model, eliminating the need for another lover ever again). Even if you are not an artist, stick figures and bad poetry will do. Read *The Vortex: Where the Law of Attraction Assembles All Cooperative Relationships* by Esther/Jerry/Abraham Hicks, and *The Soulmate Secret: Manifest the Love of Your Life with the Law of Attraction* by Arielle Ford. Or look online for creepy love spells if you wanna get weird with it, I don't judge.

Day 22

Take as much of your time that you can afford, and dedicate it to other people, scheduling a few weekly hours to seek out ways to help. Look out for charitable events in your neighbourhood that you can volunteer at (or even start your own?). Keep a list of little things you can do to be a better person and add to it whenever something else comes up. Read *The Most Good You Can Do: How Effective Altruism Is Changing Ideas About Living Ethically* by Peter Singer, *The Life You Can Save: Acting Now to End World Poverty* by Peter Singer, and *How to Change the World: Social Entrepreneurs and the Power of New Ideas* by David Bornstein.

Day 23

Please see Day 3.

Day 24

Keep working as hard as you can on every task. Start a big project or finish the one you're currently pursuing, and then immediately start another one. Look at finance books or business books or marketing books and learn how to turn yourself into a product. Make that money. Make art and sell it. Become a superhuman. Read every self-help book ever written, including *Rich Dad, Poor Dad* by Robert T. Kiyosaki and *The 48 Laws of Power* by Robert Greene.

Day 25

Research extreme sports in your area. Find out about tours of musicians or speakers you adore and try to see them in other countries. Make a bucket list or steal someone else's, by reading

1000 Places to See Before You Die Traveler's Journal (Travel Journal) by Patricia Schultz, *The Best Place to Be Today: 365 Things to Do & the Perfect Day to Do Them* by Lonely Planet, and *The Big Bucket List Book: 133 Experiences of a Lifetime* by Gin Sander. Work out a reasonable plan on how to complete everything suggested within the next decade or so.

Day 26

Write a list of all your enemies. Day by day, one by one, make amends with each individual. Refuse to have another foe ever again, even if you have to be the bigger person, in full awareness that this is your strength and their weakness. Read *The Book of Forgiving: The Fourfold Path for Healing Ourselves and Our World* by Desmond Tutu and *The Art of Forgiving* by Lewis B. Smedes.

"For the best return on your money, pour your purse into your head."
— Benjamin Franklin

It might take some time to develop your plan and source all of the materials you need (and by all means, you should give yourself that time!). But I suggest that you start each day by sparing a thought to this process, perhaps routinely in the shower or on the way to work, contemplating new and ingenious approaches to get you closer to the end goal. By doing so, your day will have a purpose, and you will move forward with the sense that you are not taking this battle lying down. You know what works for you now, so amplify it. Carry it with you after this book ends and use it to grow into a guru of your chosen field.

And I mean that quite literally. By persistently working in this constructive manner, and by researching articles/books on these topics, and by further educating yourself about heartbreak itself, and by having conversations with those who have already conquered this path, you will become the highest master of healing such pain. The expert. And people will notice. They will come to you for help, and you will know precisely how to help them. And then you have won the game.

"The more that you read, the more things you will know. The more that you learn, the more places you'll go." — Dr. Seuss

And so to recap...

Today is a personal journey which will differ from person to person. Based on your notebook or your memory, you should have a fair idea on which parts of this guide you were best at, and which you weren't. It is up to you how you wish to go forward with this information. Work on the aspects which need attention? Or strengthen the ones which you excelled at? Or both?

Take note of the chapters which were of particular interest to you, and make a plan on how to increase that vibration, preferably via the use of other literature explicitly catered to those exact needs.

Day 28
The Truth

Day 28
The Truth

"I'm extraordinarily patient provided I get my own way in the end." — Margaret Thatcher

Alright, the time has come. I'm about to blow the cap on this whole operation and expose the truth behind every day which has just passed, whether you like it or not. Are you sitting down? Hands on your underwear, ladies and gentlemen, because here we go…

There is only one proven method to heal heartbreak. *ONLY ONE.* And it's such a cliché, that I could only reveal it now otherwise I would have lost you before you'd even started the process. It's an answer so overused that you already know it, for it is as old as time itself. In fact, it is time itself. It's time. Only time can heal your broken heart.

"We must let go of the life we have planned, so as to accept the one that is waiting for us." — Joseph Campbell

Please don't throw this book away just yet, as I have more to say. But before I do, let's take a deep breath and look at this whole "time" concept rationally. When you bruise or cut yourself (accidentally, I hope), you have damaged your person. For sure, you can apply ointments, and you can seek medical advice (which is what we've been doing), but it is only through time that the body can sort its trouble out. Emotions work in the same manner, as even people who have lost someone dear to them through the natural conclusion of death, will attest to the following truth. Yes, it wasn't easy. And yes, it still hurts to think about the cause. But after enough time has passed, the crippling agony of even death can slowly dull and subside, until one gradually returns to a normal life.

These words are all easy to say, but obviously, they don't help us at all. The issue is that time slows down during periods of ache, and this is what consumes us and erodes at our quality of living. In more severe cases, time is the exact enemy, because, in its lengthy endurance, some may lose patience and make stupid decisions. Stupid decisions of which may have more permanent effects.

"Time is the longest distance between two places." — Tennessee Williams

Hence why the key is to make time move faster. And how do you do that? By distracting yourself. By removing yourself from the headspace where these wicked reminders keep nipping at your most tender memories. That way, you can propel the days forward with as little conscious investment as possible, ideally forgetting to pick at these scabs entirely.

There are various commonplace actions in which people achieve said timewarp effect following a breakup, and you have already seen them all, either in your friends or in yourself. People sleep all day; they drink until they blackout; they have sex with anyone who gives them the slightest bit of attention. Certainly, these are distractions, and yes, time will move faster during these moments.

However, the problem with these temporary blinders is that you will come crashing back into reality at some point. In this place, your heartbreak is not only still waiting for you but also comes loaded with some brand new complications. You may gain weight from lack of exercise, feel guilty for wasting money, be emotionally slaughtered from hangovers, have your self-worth deteriorated by giving up your intimacy to a stranger, or boast some nasty sexually transmitted infection. Simply put, you ran headfirst into a much bigger wall to knock yourself out for a few moments, and now you've messed your brain up even worse. You're not dealing with anything. You're shoving more stuff onto the dealing pile.

"All profound distraction opens certain doors. You have to allow yourself to be distracted when you are unable to concentrate." — Julio Cortázar, Around the Day in Eighty Worlds

And here we are, at the grand finale (even though you may have worked it out already). The overall simplified objective of this book was just that: to get you through 30 days of heartbreak by distracting you with other things. But not ordinary things. Things that you will come out holding at the other end with pride. You've turned these distractions into ways of improving your life, and as a result, have become a better person for yourself and everyone else. In essence, you have turned a bad situation into a beneficial one by emotionally profiting on what you've gone through, and there is no better way of giving yourself a high five (and someone else the middle finger). What's more, as you've built and built and built upon yourself like a bright tower made out of shiny Lego bricks, the days have passed you by, and your natural emotional healing process has begun to close the gaping wound. It works that way by design.

"Rivers know this: there is no hurry. We shall get there some day." — A.A. Milne, Winnie-the-Pooh

Now, I would never expect you to swallow such an overused pseudo-philosophy. There is nothing more tired than being told to *"find the meaning in your suffering"* or the classic *"this could be the best thing that has ever happened to you"*. It doesn't help. But, truthfully, it is still the object of the game.

I feel on some level, everyone knew this book wasn't going to be an instant fix, because how could it be? If the remedy to all heartbreak existed, I wouldn't be giving it away like this, would I? No, I would be selling it for a lot more money, and I'd be a rich man. Instead, each of us is acutely aware that the journey out of a breakup is a tough one. Because this is life, with all of its extraordinary ups and downs, beauty and pain, light and darkness. At this moment, you are currently experiencing one of the many dips in your time on Earth, surely not the first, definitely not the last. But you cannot stay down forever. The balance of the Universe will not allow for it. And each hour you kill, every smile you manage or laugh you take, achieved in a constructive manner of bettering you as a person, will be one small but definite progression in the right direction.

Mark my words on this: if not now, then one day, you will get over that person. Even if you did nothing I suggested and locked your door only to eat hot dogs for the rest of your days, eventually you would find yourself thinking of that person less until you stopped altogether (provided the hot dogs didn't kill you). Love fades and so does heartbreak, and 99.99% of you will find someone else who will come along and steal your heart. You will fall in love again, and yes, perhaps you will even get your heart broken again. It is the beauty and the tragedy of being human. It is the uncertainty of staying open to form bonds with others. And that is a risk worth taking.

"Patience is bitter, but its fruit is sweet." — Aristotle

We are two days away from completing our travels together, but as of right now, you already have all the tools you need. Perhaps some of you have escaped the hole of despair and are running forward with valour you've never harnessed before. Maybe some of you don't feel like you are in a much better place whatsoever. But for most of you, you will be somewhere in between these two points, where you are still experiencing sharp jolts of misery, yet you are notably stronger than when you first started this book. Your position on this spectrum is not the primary importance here. What is important is that you now know what to do. Distract yourself by being the best version of yourself anyone has ever seen and revel in the light that shines from you onto others. And everyone will be in awe of this impressive individual that you have become.

Finally, here is my guarantee to you. With this patience and high-speed blasting of improvements, one day, you will look back at this part of your life as one of enormous interest. Good chance, there will still be a scar, and it may be ugly, and it may be a little tender. But it may also be something you're very proud of, or even find somewhat amusing. Probably not right now, probably not tomorrow, but eventually, this will be a distant insignificant dream-like memory. And if you've utilised the upset constructively, then you could be very grateful for everything that happened. Because without it, you would not have grown into such a powerful human being.

"Only time can heal your broken heart. Just as only time can heal his broken arms and legs." — Miss Piggy

And so to recap...

Today comes with no homework and is instead a zoom-out to observe the bigger picture. The inner-workings of this life you have started to build should now be less ambiguous, allowing you to advance in ways which are even more custom by your design. It's almost exciting when we put it that way, right?

Day 29
Make Peace

Day 29
Make Peace

"Not forgiving is like drinking rat poison and then waiting for the rat to die." — Anne Lamott, Traveling Mercies: Some Thoughts on Faith

Today's task is perhaps one you are not quite ready for, and that is ok. Only you know your circumstances, and you should use these suggestions at your discretion. But at some point, you may want to consider the unfathomable idea of making peace with your ex and the breakup situation, even if it takes place in your head and you don't get them involved whatsoever.

Let's analyse what this may entail by looking back at where we have come. If you've been following this book's instructions correctly, my proposals should be a part of your daily procedure, and you should have cut off all contact with your ex.

For some of you, you achieved this with a badge of honour and did not speak to them for roughly a month. I bow to you if that is the case.

For others, this was an unreasonable request. Still, I hope you took my consultation as best you could, keeping the exchanges brief and purposeful, avoiding any emotional blabberings and ensuring the talk was strictly business. That will have also worked just fine.

But for those of you who faltered and spoke to your ex at regular intervals, then, unfortunately, this step will be lost on you. It is a pity, but don't beat yourself up about it because what's done is done and it is what it is. Read this chapter anyway, and perhaps you will still find something of use, albeit substantially diluted.

"Forgive your enemies, but never forget their names."
— John F. Kennedy

You should also have a list in your possession, one that you've been slowly compiling throughout this book. The said list should consist of the various unresolved questions or bitter spews of hatred or anything you would like to tell your ex, but (hopefully) have not done so just yet. *(this list was initiated on Day 4, if you need a reference point).*

These two steps meet, and end, right now.

"It's not a person's mistakes which define them - it's the way they make amends." — Freya North, Chances

Maybe it's not today. Maybe it is. But there will come a time when you can no longer justify this grudge. And when that time comes, you must be fully equipped to drop all of this weight in one sudden move—everything, all at once.

The key to do this is to look over those random pending thoughts and confusions you've been writing down then connect them, building one coherent speech or letter. This speech/letter will serve as everything you want to say and need to know, in one cohesive article.

"It's so hard to forget pain, but it's even harder to remember sweetness. We have no scar to show for happiness. We learn so little from peace." — Chuck Palahniuk; Diary

But here lies the deeper value of this step: write it from a place of love and forgiveness. Word each question and perplexing contemplation as politely and as calmly as you can muster. Pretend your words will reach their (or even your) mother. Try to remember the good things about them. Recall the reasons why you got along in the first place. Grant them the benefit of certain doubts. Put yourself in their shoes. Be fair and identify where you went wrong. Try as hard as you can to focus on the lessons they taught you about yourself (as well as relationships in general). It may even help you to write from a third-person viewpoint, removing yourself from the story, becoming an observer in a speech written by the fictional character you wish you were.

Do not rush this. If you are not ready to stare directly at the fiery sun within your heart, then use today to read over what you already have. Contemplate how you would word it better. And then gradually approach this exercise in your own time. Take today as far as you feel capable.

If/When you manage to form an orderly, comprehensive, civilised letter/speech, then read it out loud in the mirror. Feel the burn. Then decide what you want to do with it. Perhaps you honestly never want to see or hear from this person again, and then hopefully this act alone will be enough to find some peace in your gut. The detailing of the complete story. One well-rounded essay with a beginning, a middle, and an end. A place where you can now step back and look at it exactly as it is: a chapter in the book of your life. A segment you can forgive and leave behind without having to make contact ever again, ready to turn to the next page, writing something new.

"True forgiveness is when you can say, "'Thank you for that experience.'" — Oprah Winfrey

However, now that you've strung together all of your queries and statements in a constructive, linear fashion, you may feel it is time to reopen the doors of communications and make amends with this individual personally (even if you were in the wrong). Have you reached this place of strength? Do you think you can handle the outcome, whatever it might be? Then type your statement in an email, or make a plan to meet up, rehearsing your lines so that you can get everything off of your chest at once. *BUT* (and this is a big *BUT*), do remember that there is a massive risk involved here. Unsealing these tombs again could erode all of your hard work, so you must think carefully and clearly about your intentions before even considering this move.

If you have fantasies about your magical words getting you back together with your ex, or provoking an emotional reaction, or rubbing their face in everything that they have done wrong, then I am sorry to say, but you are not ready. Reread yesterday's step, and then re-approach this later. Because such a misguided aim will almost inevitably turn into an argument where you lose all of your acquired cool. It will backfire, and send you spinning sideways a long distance behind from how far you have come.

But if your intentions blossom from a place of wanting to let go of this pain, to find peace in your life, or perhaps to even revitalise the strong friendship you once shared, then you are ready. Rehearse today's letter until you know it by heart, then go forth with your brilliantly crafted words. Explain yourself quietly, honestly, and respectfully, then grant them time to explain themselves. Be decent, and make peace. If you find they are still that same person, then take in a breath of solace, knowing that you've done all you can. You've said all you have to say. Turn around, and walk away from this situation, forever.

"The weak can never forgive. Forgiveness is the attribute of the strong."
— Mahatma Gandhi

Do not try to fool yourself. Reconnecting these lines of transmission will sting and could unravel some of the progress you've achieved recently. In that same thought, it could also be the most crucial step in finding closure. You may finally wrap it up in a box and move on, especially if they haven't changed at all when your life has grown so much in the last 29 days. Best case scenario, you remember who they really are without the heartbreak tinted glasses, realising that the personality you'd developed and obsessed over was of your creation. This discovery will further solidify why your relationship did not work in the first place. I hope this is the case for you, as this was the case for me.

On the flip side, there are situations where you may feel this person does not deserve forgiveness, and that is fine too. There are also those cases where you may think you don't deserve forgiveness, and in regards to this exercise, that is also fine. But you should still approach this concept with your full attention because, as we spoke about on Day 26, harbouring a grudge is not harming anyone except for yourself.

"You know, it's funny. When you look at someone through rose-coloured glasses, all the red flags just look like flags."
— Wanda Pierce

Finally, please allow me to remind you of something. It is not down to us to forgive an individual or even ourselves. The reason is that we are not some godlike authority figure who has the power to decide who deserves forgiveness or not. Instead, the desperate claws which cling onto animosity do not even touch this person, for they are not feeling what you are feeling. You are, in reality, only hurting yourself. Forgiving a person has nothing to do with them. It has everything to do with you. And for that reason, do yourself a favour, and work towards making peace with this story. Not for me, or them, or anyone else. For you.

"Sometimes you only get one chance to rewrite the qualities of the character you played in a person's life story. Always take it. Never let the world read the wrong version of you." — Shannon L. Alder

And so to recap...

Today the time has finally come to group all of your unresolved thoughts and unanswered questions together and write them out in a coherent, articulate speech. What you do with this is up to you. But the main goal is to find closure in your words, forgiveness in your mind, and peace in your heart.

Perhaps this won't happen today, but it's time to face in that direction, and step toward it, one foot at a time, for yourself.

Day 30
Goodbye

Day 30
Goodbye

"Sometimes a little heartbreak is a lesson, and the best thing to do is just learn the lesson." — Jon Voight

And that's it! You have reached the end of this book! You read the whole thing! Which, if nothing else, is something you can be proud of. This achievement proves you have a healthy level of commitment and determination. And, sometimes, that's all we need.

Now I am fully aware that some of my readers will not have done everything (or anything?) I suggested, because I, at times, have treated self-help books in the same manner. It is also possible that you broke the careful structure I had so meticulously planned for you, and didn't follow this book day-by-day. Shame on you! If either of these scenarios rings true for your case, then I can't send you off properly because we didn't meet halfway. But I can wish you well, in hopes that you got something or other out of the experience.

For everyone else, I will be spending our final moments together with the assumption that you did everything I proposed, and you have arrived at this point ready for our planned farewell.

"I think heartbreak is something that you learn to live with as opposed to learn to forget." — Kate Winslet

First of all, please turn back to Day 2 of your notebook, and look at the list you made, reading those points you were hoping to achieve during the last month. How did you do? What was your final score? I would never expect anyone to get 100% full marks, but with a bit of luck and perseverance, maybe you look back on it with a certain sense of accomplishment (or at least amusement). Furthermore, those hopes you wrote down and didn't quite manage to complete are valuable too. You can use them to diagnose the weaker links in your chain of ambition and then work on those as you venture out into the wild all by yourself.

Moving forward, and it would be impossible for me to address every reader in one foolproof blanket statement, as I imagine feelings about the breakup will still vary from person to person. And so, let's put those thoughts aside for one quick moment, and instead reflect at what you *have* managed to do, or at least tried to do, which is all anyone could reasonably ask.

You started by making a conscious effort to stand up, refusing to surrender to these feelings, simply by picking up this book. But you also did so by pulling out a notepad and documenting your progress, using this time to reevaluate the situation, turning it into a mission of evolution, and taking each step necessary to jump over this barrier, no matter how far you got.

You claimed responsibility for your emotions, spending many days pondering the things you have done and the things you have failed to do.

You explored ways to better climb an emotional ladder towards more potent energy, the concept of progression perpetually on your mind (because I insisted on reminding you).

You exorcised your negativity by constructively transferring it from your crowded mind onto paper. It now exists in a tangible place in the physical world, which will always be there. It's a massive bundle of unique inner chaos, spat out in your own words, perhaps even via an artistic medium, filled with passion and pain, forever in your possession as a reflection of this weird stage in your life.

You made the decision (at whatever degree) to maturely handle your ex's presence in your life, placing a safe distance between you and them and their negative influence, training yourself to take control of what you are willing to deal with every day.

You spoke to your friends regularly, not only in an attempt to dump your troubles onto their heads, but to also find comfort in their guiding advice, cautiously avoiding the temptation of being a draining downer who bad mouths people. You offered your mates the chance to be neutral on the matter, and ultimately, you came across as the bigger person.

You did not write off (or perhaps even embraced) the idea of getting professional help. Therapy is arguably the bravest (and often most successful) step a person can take, admitting they are in a messy situation for which they don't have the solution.

You reconsidered intoxicating your troubles away, ideally minimising (or eradicating) the intake of any mind-altering substances. This one move can grant your head a running start through the clear, tackling your troubles with all the mental strength you can muster.

You exercised some apprehension towards the temporary affection of others and created a personal space where you needed to love yourself without using any external touch to validate your worth. Or maybe you didn't, but at least you thought about it, right?

You revamped your appearance, now looking like a brand new person since you started this book, a makeover which altered people's perception of you while improving your confidence every time you looked in the mirror. Hey there, sexy stranger.

You treated your room and house in much the same manner, reconstructing a brand new habitat by building a new environment, absent of painful memories, coming home to a place that no longer reflected an outdated period of your life. Furthermore, you began to clean and tidy everything up, organising your material world, which gave you purpose and hygienic spaces for your thoughts.

You inspected your routine, contemplating ways you could speed up the machine whilst also dressing it up differently, forever altering your dull practices by testing small changes, jolting your brain away from the familiarity of mundane responsibilities. It's all about spontaneity, making decisions to get a little further out of your regular comfort zone, and keeping your mind on its toes.

You explored the importance of putting *you* first and indulging your pleasures once in a while, enjoying things that speak to your happiness, making friends with the self within yourself. A peace offering of sorts. In this way, you learned not to be too strict on your recovery or to take this whole process too seriously.

Furthermore, you should have pulled more of your health on board, finding time for physical activity no matter how small, cultivating the happy chemicals your body deserves whilst firming up your hotness levels too.

You also approached this idea from the dietary angle, consuming better food to fuel your mind towards liberation, and granting you the energy required to take each day, one at a time.

You looked inwards at the vibrations of your being, trying to quieten down your racing mind either employing prayer or meditation or by merely unplugging for a while and numbing your contemplations, focusing upon external distractions to divert any painful pangs.

You compiled a list of reasons why you are a good person and a perfect catch for someone out there because, no matter what your faults are, you were able to recognise that you possess qualities that other people do not. And it is these specific excellences, the ones which are stitched into your core, that someone else is looking for, without fail.

You then designed that very person from scratch, the exact human who would match these ideal qualities. You now have the foresight of what you seek, refusing to settle for anything less than what you deserve.

You learned the value of helping others as the fastest way to become an asset to the world, all the while dousing your troubles in perspective gasoline then flicking the match of emotional reward to set it ablaze!

You faced the idea of putting your heart and soul into your profession and your hobbies, progressing yourself into a better worker, carrying an improved set of tools, climbing up the ladder of success, and becoming a resource of further importance. In other words, a much more desired person from all walks of life.

You learned that if you were ever in a place of emotional distress, all you had to do was approach something scarier than the fear you already carry. With this, you would intentionally overpower the stress immediately, taking risky leaps forward and leaving the small stuff behind.

You learned to forgive others, even if they were in the wrong or did not deserve it. Because forgiveness is about empowering yourself whilst mending unnecessarily broken wiring, slowly building a warmer community of love around you, and practising the art of letting insignificant details go.

You took a long look hard at your brain throughout this whole book, locating where your most significant flaws and strengths are, using this information to improve certain areas in hopes of one day becoming the best in the world!

You began to grasp patience as your greatest ally, and by diving headfirst into as many useful distractions as possible, you could turn this terrible time into something that will advance you as a person. Ultimately (and inevitably) this whole nightmare will fall behind you as a ledge—one which was challenging to climb on top of, certainly, but from where you stand... the view is incredible.

And finally, you have started to make the final steps towards dusting yourself off and releasing the grip which has been holding you back this whole time. Your ex. Perhaps one day, you will make peace with them and within yourself. Perhaps you never will. But what matters is this: if you've thought about the topic all you can, then it is time to let go and move on. How you manage to do this, is up to you.

"Life has got all those twists and turns. You've got to hold on tight and off you go." — Nicole Kidman

Some of those above lessons may have resonated with you, and some may have not. Do not worry about anything, ever. For as I said before, nobody will boast the perfect score, and that was never the point anyway. You should use your final day to decide how you want to approach whatever you see fit. If you felt a jitter of excitement about any of those spoken achievements or you remember days of particular benefit, then perhaps that is where your priorities should lie going forward. Or maybe, specific points previously mentioned gave you a small dull thud of disappointment, saddened that you didn't quite reach where you wanted to go. And that's fine too. You can leave it, or you can work on it, whatever makes you feel the most comfortable. Here, take the steering wheel, you are in complete control now.

"We must be willing to let go of the life we planned so as to have the life that is waiting for us." — Joseph Campbell

But whichever way you go, hold your head up high. You have put the time and effort into something significant in your life. That alone confirms you as a person of much integrity and worth, significantly more than those who (in a similar situation) would let the pain consume and immobilise them. Some people choose to writhe in misery. They do nothing but delay the inescapable fact that heartbreak will always die down, and then they are left to deal with the mess that they created along their path of destruction. But not you. You took this depressed platform and turned it to your powerful advantage, and even if your heart still aches, you are already a much better person because of it.

"Life is like riding a bicycle. To keep your balance, you must keep moving." — Albert Einstein

What happens now is not up to me to even guess. Some of you may fall backwards into a dark cloud once again because there won't be this daily guidance to keep your purpose mobile. If this happens, then let it happen. Give your brain the time to churn and deal with the breakup using the equipment it has learned from what I've taught you. And just know that this too will pass. Alternatively, you could always reread the book? It'll be fun, you'll see! I'll pretend I don't even know you, so it's like we're meeting for the first time!

On the other hand, some of you may find that you're further over the ex than you thought you would be. The idea of this person was better than the reality. It's not that you miss *them*, but more that you miss the filling in your life that they provided and it's the hole left behind that hurts. Their absence. Nothing to do with their personality. And as you have built up this momentum in the last month, propelling you forward, becoming the best version of yourself… and as they have stayed still, not improving at the same drastic rate that you have... then it's easy to see that going back to them would be a stupid move. It would be a move in the opposite direction.

"Sometimes you will never know the value of a moment, until it becomes a memory." — Dr. Seuss

Before we finally part ways, I would like to share one last trick with you. Arguably the best weapon against my anguish was found during the process of writing this very book. And not from the step-by-step instruction basis either. Instead, it was by writing the damn thing itself. I wrote so extensively about my loss, delved so deep into my personal pit of despair, and pedantically researched so many other people's misfortune, that eventually the very concept of heartbreak bored me right out of my skin. The tiring monotony of articulating heartache every single damn day eventually made me feel indifferent. It desensitised me to my feelings until I was cured beyond the point of caring about being cured.

And so, if you are in need of one final desperate ploy to escape the clawed fingers of a loveless sorrow, then write a book about it. Before you know it, your problems will become so dull that you will have no choice other than to move on.

Best of luck to you. You got this.

"I may not have gone where I intended to go, but I think I have ended up where I needed to be." — Douglas Adams; The Long Dark Tea-Time of the Soul

HEARTBREAK SUCKS!

how to get over your breakup in 30 days

You Can Be the Hero of this Story!

Thank you for reading *Heartbreak Sucks!* By purchasing this book, you have helped me to write for another day! However, if you seek to spread more healing throughout the world, there is a way to assist further, and it won't cost you a penny!

You see, Amazon's algorithm is an extremely intelligent beast that judges authors' products based on many factors. But inarguably, our most significant power comes from **verified reviews**. So when you take a few minutes to tell the world what you thought of this book, the website wakes up and lifts the title to higher eyes, feeding itself in the process. The author has no control over this side of the deal. It entirely relies on you!

Hence, please consider reviewing *Heartbreak Sucks!* You wouldn't believe the difference a single rating makes.

Thank you again so very much!
Lots of love,
Jared Woods

Amazon Link:
https://mybook.to/heartbreaksucks

About the Author

Born in South Africa and now homeless as a nomadic something or other, Jared Woods does whatever he wants. He is best known as the former scriptwriter for the YouTube channel *Pencilmation*, where billions of people have seen his work with scripts surpassing the 100 million mark.

Heartbreak Sucks! is just one of numerous books Jared has authored. Others include the dating app self-help publication *Swiping Right*, the fictional collection *Licking the Bottom of the Love Jar,* and the music journalism piece *F**ked My Way Up to the Top: The Complete Biography of Lana Del Rey*. But most importantly, we have Jared's own spiritual philosophy, the *Janthopoyism Bible*. Get that first.

Further creative projects include the one-panel Instagram comic *#legobiscuits*, his solo music under the name *Coming Down Happy*, his "singing" for the band *Sectlinefor*, and his film production called *Definitely Not a Cry For Help* which is already partially on YouTube.

Visit Jared at *Jared Woods Saved My Life.com*
Follow Jared on *Instagram*, *Twitter*, and *Threads* ***@legotrip***

Other Books by Jared Woods

F**ked My Way Up to the Top: The Complete Biography of Lana Del Rey Using Her Own Words (2023)
Licking the Bottom of the Love Jar (2023)
Swiping Right (2023)
Janthopoyism Bible (2022)
This Is Your Brain On Drugs (2016)

Made in the USA
Las Vegas, NV
09 March 2024

86946158R00125